MANUAL
ON
PREACHING

MANUAL
ON
PREACHING

Milton Crum, Jr.

A New Process of Sermon Development

MOREHOUSE-BARLOW
Wilton, Connecticut

MANUAL ON PREACHING

Versions of the Bible quoted in this volume are:

The Holy Bible, King James Version.

The Revised Standard Version of the Bible, copyrighted 1952 and 1971 by the Division of Christian Education of the National Council of the Churches of Christ in the United States of America. Used by permission.

The Jerusalem Bible. Copyright Doubleday & Company, Inc., 1966.

Today's English Version, the GOOD NEWS BIBLE—Old Testament: copyright © American Bible Society 1976; New Testament: copyright © American Bible Society 1966, 1971, 1976. Used by permission.

The Amplified New Testament. By permission of The Lockman Foundation.

The Complete Bible, an American Translation, by J. M. P. Smith and E. J. Goodspeed. Copyright 1931 by the University of Chicago. Used by permission.

The Bible: A New Translation. Copyright 1954 by James Moffatt, by permission of Harper & Row, Publishers, Inc.

The New English Bible. © The Delegates of the Oxford University Press and The Syndics of the Cambridge University Press, 1961, 1970.

Library of Congress Cataloging-in-Publication Data

Crum, Milton.
    Manual on preaching.

    Bibliography: p.
    Includes index.
    1. Preaching. I. Title.
BV4211.2.C78   1988   251   88-5159
ISBN 0-8192-1459-0 (pbk.)

Printed in the United States of America
by
BSC Litho, Harrisburg, PA

In gratitude to
Richard C. Hoefler,
who taught me to preach;
John Q. Beckwith,
who taught me to teach;
the students and parishioners,
who challenged and enabled me
to write this manual.

"A rabbi, whose grandfather had been a disciple of the Baal Shem, was asked to tell a story. 'A story,' he said, 'must be told in such a way that it constitutes help in itself.' And he told: 'My grandfather was lame. Once they asked him to tell a story about his teacher. And he related how the holy Baal Shem used to hop and dance while he prayed. My grandfather rose as he spoke, and he was so swept away by his story that he himself began to hop and dance to show how the master had done. From that hour on he was cured of his lameness. That's the way to tell a story!'"*

*Martin Buber, *Tales of the Hasidim: The Early Masters* (New York: Schocken Books, Inc., 1947), pp. v-vi.

PREFACE

Milton Crum has broken new ground in the literature of Christian preaching. He has taken seriously the difficulty of moving from the text to the sermon and, with remarkable clarity, has offered concrete help to the learner.

Motivating his task is the frustration of uncounted generations of persons engaged in pulpit communication. Seminary professors of Bible and theology hear recent alumni preach in their parishes as if they had never set foot in a theological school; they are hurt and angry. Homiletics professors search hungrily for a way to help students achieve what their colleagues in the biblical field do not always do—to help students discover the meaning of biblical materials for the contemporary scene. Seminary students, caught uneasily between the nuances of textual criticism and the cries of lonely teenagers in their field education assignment, wonder if they will ever be able to connect the two. Parish pastors have too often given up on the attempt to preach biblical-contemporary sermons.

Perhaps the person who suffers most is the pew-sitter who is living out a life of pain, fundamentally untouched by the healing of the gospel. The "gospel" may be read, alluded to in the course of the sermon, invoked as a blessing at worship's end, but the worshiper never personally moves to the center of the gospel story. The fault may be hers or his, betraying a lack of intelligence or interest. It may rather be the preacher's, who has never really understood the pulpit's job to be the retelling of the gospel story so as to involve the congregation in it, at the deepest level.

Regretfully, the homiletical search is too often for three points, or a listing of virtues to be emulated, or even the raising of important issues with which the church must deal. Too seldom does the preacher begin the preparation of the sermon with the fundamental question, what is going on in the lives of the people who hear me? Whether that question surfaces before or after the choice of a text, it must inevitably lead to the gospel, to the Christ who is at work redemptively in human experience.

Professor Crum comes at his task with a keen sensitivity to the human situation and also with an ear to biblical scholarship. Without getting lost in the thicket of technical problems, he alerts the reader to the biblical message which comes through searching critical study. He also leads the reader into the most exciting part of the widely current discussion of theology as story.

The most delightful part of this book is that it works! Lectures on preaching, committed to print, are sometimes grand and inspirational reading, but it is the rare reader who can translate their insights into the structures and the style of next Sunday's sermon. The how-to-do-it books tend toward the simplistic, the theologically vapid. This book successfully straddles the world of the scholarly and the practical. The homiletical community, teachers and preachers alike, are in Professor Crum's debt.

William D. Thompson
Professor of Preaching
Eastern Baptist Theological Seminary
Philadelphia, Pennsylvania

FOREWORD

My *purpose* in writing the book is to assist preachers in actually doing preaching. Therefore, I have tried to bring together a *how* (or method) and a *why* (or rationale) for preaching the gospel.

I have tried to make the *how* of the method practical and specific enough to enable a beginner to do the whole sermon process from Bible study to designing and preaching a sermon to discerning its effectiveness in worship and society.

I have tried to make the *why* of the rationale theoretical and general enough to stretch the minds of more experienced preachers and to encourage experimentation with the method.

My *sources* for the book are twofold. In twenty-five years of ordained ministry and ten years of teaching homiletics, I have preached and listened to several thousand sermons. These sermons and listener responses to them have provided my basic data source. From this data I have tried to identify elements in sermon design and delivery which enhance communication of the gospel. For help in identifying these elements, my source has been study in the fields of general semantics, communication and behavior, and homiletics. After identifying the elements which enhance communication of the gospel, I have tried to put them together as a unified method and rationale for preaching the gospel.

Milton Crum, Jr.
Protestant Episcopal Theological
Seminary in Virginia

CONTENTS

Chapter 1

AN INTRODUCTION
TO THE MANUAL
AND ITS METHOD

*This chapter contains an introduction to both the
manual and the preaching method which it describes.*

"I've got to preach next week." You may say this in reference to
your first sermon in Homiletics One or in reference to your three-
hundredth sermon in the same church. But, always, there is that
empty "space" in thought and time which must be filled with words.

My work with students and congregations has convinced me
that, in effective preaching, the words with which that "space" is filled
do two things. First, the words describe an aspect of our human
situation (which in a fallen world always needs some remedying) so
you and the congregation can identify with the description and say,
"That's me, O Lord, standing in need of the gospel." Secondly, the
words communicate something of the gospel of what God has done
for us in Jesus Christ, so God may speak his Word through the words
of the sermon to remedy the aspect of the human situation under
focus. Then you and the congregation can rejoice and say, "Thank
God."

Purpose of the Manual

The purpose of the method described in this manual is to

facilitate filling sermon "space" with words which will bring about change and evoke thanksgiving in the preacher and also, it is hoped, in the congregation. The manual, as the word implies, is unashamedly a how-to-do-it book. It presents a method of sermon development which I have learned from a combination of observing methods which have produced effective sermons in ten years of teaching homiletics classes and of reading about preaching, Bible, and communication studies.

I know the method works well in developing sermons by which to preach the gospel movingly, for I have used it and seen it used many times. The difficulty lies in describing the process with sufficient detail to enable the reader to do what is being described without getting bogged down in too many details. You may recall the difficulty of writing a paper on "How to Tie Your Shoelaces" in English composition. Describing how to do it is more difficult than actually doing the process.

The method is intended to be sufficiently defined

1. to focus your initial attention on the Bible and to engage you in thinking in biblical structures of thought, and

2. to focus your corollary attention on your own life, and then that of your congregation, not only on the level of symptomatic behavior, but also at the deeper level of the roots of behavior, so that you and your congregation may receive in mind and heart the power of the gospel, and

3. to order your thinking so you can design the sermon as a story which you can tell with clarity and with feeling. At the same time, the method is intended to be sufficiently undefined in order to allow room for the marvelous and creative ways in which insights may happen to you in the process of listening through Scripture and designing a sermon.

Biblical Grounding

The manual seeks to facilitate preaching which is like telling a clear and simple, person-to-person story of human change effected by the gospel of God's holy love. The preacher will have experienced the story through the Scripture as a prerequisite to being able to tell the story as a sermon. During the telling of the sermon, the preacher will experience it again, and it is hoped that the hearers will also experience the sermon so they, too, may be moved in heart and mind and thus be changed a bit more into the fullness of Christ.

Biblical Understanding of the People to Whom We Preach

Every preacher approaches preaching with at least a tacit understanding of human behavior and how to affect it. If the approach is moralistic, the preacher will tell those in the congregation how they ought to behave. If the approach is idealistic, the preacher will hold up ideals for behavior, which, if the people would emulate them, would make life happier.

What the moralistic preacher says people ought to do may be right. It may also be true that if people behaved according to the ideals which the idealistic preacher prescribes, life would be happier. The problem is that moralistic and idealistic preaching are generally ineffective in changing human behavior, for they address only symptoms and not the roots of behavior. Only a change in the inner person, in the person's heart and mind, can effect a voluntary change in symptomatic behavior. Recall Jesus' teaching that a tree bears fruit according to the kind of tree it is, and a person acts according to his or her heart (Matthew 7:17-18; Luke 6:43-45); or Paul's teaching that the branches of a tree are according to its root (Romans 11:16). A functional picture of the biblical understanding of the person to whom we preach might look like this:

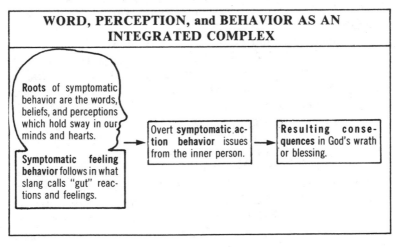

WORD, PERCEPTION, and BEHAVIOR AS AN INTEGRATED COMPLEX

Roots of symptomatic behavior are the words, beliefs, and perceptions which hold sway in our minds and hearts.

Symptomatic feeling behavior follows in what slang calls "gut" reactions and feelings.

Overt **symptomatic action behavior** issues from the inner person.

Resulting consequences in God's wrath or blessing.

A person can no more voluntarily act contrary to the root beliefs and perceptions which dominate his or her mind and heart than can an evil tree bear good fruit or a good tree bear evil fruit. Therefore, the manual will suggest a dynamic for getting at the roots of symptomatic behavior and addressing them with the gospel in hope of producing change. Such preaching is more difficult than moralistic or idealistic preaching, but it is the more biblical and the more effective way.

The Bible, the Preacher, and the Sermon as Story

The preacher is one of the persons to whom the sermon is preached. If the sermon is to speak effectively to the preacher, it will grow out of his or her experience of being personally moved by study of the Scripture on which the sermon is based. The Scripture provides the words and images, and the relationships between them, which serve as clues for identifying some symptomatic behavior in the preacher's life which needs the therapy of the gospel. These also become clues to the gospel content which speaks to the root of the behavior.

If the sermon describes an aspect of life which is deficient in the gospel so vividly that the preacher must say, "That's me, O Lord, standing in need of the gospel," it is likely that other people will respond that way, too. If the sermon affirms the gospel with such credibility that the preacher can say, "Thank God," it is likely that other people will, too.

A sermon which moves from an area of life standing in need of the gospel to that area of life as transformed by the gospel has the basic characteristics of a story. A human story begins somewhere in human life and moves somewhere, and the movement makes a significant difference. Such a sermon, like any story, will include (1) verbal content, (2) a structure, and (3) a dynamic.

1. The *verbal content* of the sermon will be grounded in Scripture, which will provide the words and images which help both preacher and listener "see" what is being said. Too often a preacher fills a sermon with verbal content which the preacher already knows and then seeks a text to validate what the preacher wants to say. Such preaching may be biblical to the extent that the preacher thinks biblically. But the new insights into human life and the fresh nuances

of the gospel which are given through the study of Scripture, often through the least likely passages, will be missed. The preacher who does not listen to God through Scripture must either run dry or preach a gospel other than the gospel of God.

Use of the Bible, as the primary clue for the sermon's content, will be illustrated in chapters 2 and 3 and developed conceptually in chapter 4.

2. The *structure* of sermons may be as varied as the structures of stories, but all stories build movement into their structures. Sermons, like the biblical story, will move from fallen humanity to redeemed humanity, from sin to faith, from darkness to light, from what Paul calls living "according to the flesh" to living "according to the spirit," from condemnation to justification, from alienation to sanctification. This movement will not only be incorporated in the verbal structure of the sermon, but it will also be an experiential movement in the mind and heart of the preacher and, it is hoped, in the minds and hearts of the congregation.

In order to experience the structural movement of the sermon, the preacher must know what the words mean in his or her own life. This may require that the preacher experience the pain of facing unsavory aspects of his or her life. It may require the anguish of doubting the very gospel which the preacher desperately needs to believe.

Preaching which incorporates experiential movement demands greater personal investment by the preacher than does preaching about a topic. A preacher can get several points to make about a topic, such as faith or grace, from books and deliver them in a sermon without ever becoming personally involved. When this is done, it is unlikely that either the preacher or the congregation will be moved by the sermon. In contrast, biblical preaching so moves preacher and congregation in the fashion that Paul spoke of as faith being engendered by preaching (Romans 10:17) and Peter spoke of as being born anew by preaching (1 Peter 1:23-25).

The story-like structure of the sermon is illustrated in chapters 2 and 3 and developed conceptually in chapter 5.

3. If the sermon is to move the listener, not only must the verbal content be structured with movement, but the verbal content must also contain *Dynamic Factors* which facilitate the movement.

The factor which is usually the most obvious and the easiest for the preacher to develop is a description of some commonly experienced *symptomatic behavior* which needs to be changed by the gospel. This factor is a concrete example of our fallen, sinful behavior. The behavior, on the feeling and/or action level, is described with such concrete detail and pastoral empathy that a listener can say, "That's me; I behave that way," without fear of condemnation.

Less obvious and requiring more pastoral and theological insight is the Dynamic Factor which gets at the *root* of the symptomatic behavior under focus. This factor sets forth the beliefs and perceptions which underlie the behavior. This is the area of the inner person: the mind which needs renewing (Romans 12:2), the heart which needs to be filled with good treasure (Luke 6:45), and the old nature which needs to be replaced by a new one (Ephesians 4:22-24). When the underlying root of the symptomatic behavior is described vividly and empathetically, the listener can respond, "That's me; that is why I act that way."

In the biblical story, the wrath of God does not allow us to behave sinfully with impunity. The unhappy *resulting consequences* which follow sinful behavior are, in faith, understood as God's wrath reaching out to change us. A recounting of these unhappy consequences of our sinful behavior conveys the message that we ought not behave that way much more effectively than moralistic exhortation ever could. In addition, identifying God's wrath in the consequences of sinful behavior serves to shake us loose from that way of living. Therefore, the purpose of this Dynamic Factor is to bring a person to say, "That's me; that's what happens when I behave that way; I would like to be able to behave differently."

Even though the unhappy consequences, which the symptomatic behavior under focus produces, may press the person to desire change, the person is unable to change behavior until the mind and heart, in which the behavior is rooted, are changed. To accomplish this change, the Dynamic Factor of *gospel content* offers an alternative to the old way of believing and perceiving. At this point, many preachers fall into either moralism or idealism, rather than boldly and explicitly speaking the gospel of God. Contrary to Paul, many preachers seem to be ashamed to speak the gospel boldly as the foundation for their lives (Romans 1:16). Maybe they are afraid of looking foolish by personally testifying to "the foolishness of God" (1 Corinthians 1:25). Too often preachers shy away from direct affirmations, such as, "Not even death can separate us from the love of God," or "By his action on the cross, God makes us righteous, even though by our own actions we are unrighteous." Nevertheless, when the gospel is proclaimed, people respond, "Thank God for the gospel which gives me a new way of believing and perceiving."

The last Dynamic Factor is the *new results* which follow the new way of believing and perceiving which the gospel provides. The new results include new symptomatic behavior on the feeling and/or action levels and new consequences which follow as obedience to faith (Romans 16:26). When the new results are experienced as the result of awareness of the old consequences coupled with release by the gospel, rather than as a new moralism or idealism, the listener can respond, "Thank God, who by his word both wills and works in us for his good pleasure" (see Philippians 2:13).

When these five Dynamic Factors are incorporated into the sermon story, the story is imbued with the power to move hearts and minds. How to incorporate the Dynamic Factors into the sermon is illustrated in chapters 2 and 3, and they are developed conceptually in chapter 6.

Using the Manual

The manual follows a progression from the more concrete to the more conceptual. Chapter 2, "Preaching the Gospel: An Overview," touches on everything in the manual while narrating the development and delivery of an actual sermon. Chapter 3 zooms in on sermon development with two more detailed examples. Chapters 4, 5, and 6 present aspects of sermon development more conceptually, namely, "Biblical Interpretation," "Synopsis of the Sermon," and "Dynamics of the Sermon." The last two chapters present additional aspects of the sermon in the context of worship and theology.

Many parts are detailed accounts of a thought process for developing sermons. Such detail makes for tedious reading, but such detail also makes it possible for the reader to do the kind of preaching which the manual proposes. Most books on preaching hold up homiletical ideals without setting forth a practical process for achieving the ideal. The purpose of this manual is to enable you to follow the process it describes, so that you can adapt the method for your own needs.

Simply reading the manual cannot bring about the kind of preaching it envisions any more than swimming or sailing or counseling can be learned by simply reading a book. Trying to put the method into practice, step by step, and testing the results are essential if you want to preach the gospel as the manual proposes. A manual is for *doing* as well as for reading.

Chapter 2

PREACHING THE GOSPEL: AN OVERVIEW

This chapter recounts the development and delivery of an actual sermon and elucidates some of the rationale for what was done. The reader should pay more attention to the PROCESS being exemplified than to the sermon being used as the example. (A transcript of the sermon is appended to the chapter.)

In order to present an overview of the preaching method which this manual presents, I will recount the development and delivery of an actual sermon and elucidate some of the rationale for what I did. The sermon was preached at a regular Sunday service without any intention of using it as a case study.

The first draft of this chapter was written in response to questions raised in a lay sermon group about what a preacher thinks he or she is about in preaching and what a preacher aims for in preaching. I hope that readers of this manual will be challenged to write their responses to these questions and share them with their congregations for discussion.[1]

Power of Preaching

Preaching, like all communication, has been in trouble ever since

Babel, when "the LORD confused the language of all the earth" (Genesis 11:9, RSV).

In Jeremiah, God denounced the false prophets who spoke lies in his name and stole words from one another, like those who use "canned" sermons so widely today (Jeremiah 23).

Paul's preaching once sparked a riot which endangered his life, and his carefully planned Athens sermon received mixed responses: "some mocked" and "some . . . believed" (Acts 17:32-34; 19:23-41).

In a Lenten sermon, St. Augustine complained about the "mere handful" in church and the larger numbers "who now fill theaters."

A sixteenth-century survey of what people wanted in sermons discovered that

> Some would have long texts:
> some short texts.
> Some would have it ordered by Logic:
> some term that man's wisdom.
> Some would have it polished by Rhetoric:
> some call it persuasibleness of words.
> Some love study and learning in Sermons:
> some allow only a sudden motion of the spirit.
> Some would have all said by heart:
> some would have recourse made often to the book.
> Some love gestures:
> some no gestures.
> Some love long Sermons:
> some short Sermons.
> Some are coy, and can brook no Sermons at all.[2]

In July, 1851, the noted English preacher, Frederick W. Robertson, lamented:

> . . . by the change of times the pulpit has lost its place. It does only part of that whole which used to be done by it alone. Once it was newspaper, schoolmaster, theological treatise, a stimulant to good works, historical lecture, metaphysics, etc., all in one. Now these are partitioned out to different officers, and the pulpit is no more the pulpit of three centuries back . . .[3]

Yet, words are our primary communication medium; and, in spite of all the difficulties with language and preaching, the words of Jeremiah and Paul and Augustine and Robertson and countless other preachers still turn minds and hearts toward Jesus Christ.

The power of preaching to move people is demonstrated by the response to the sermon which I am using as the case in point for this chapter. The sermon certainly could not be called a great one. It is a sermon which could have been preached by any seminary student or pastor. Yet the response, both written and oral, indicated a powerful effect. As evidence, one of the feedback sheets reads as follows:

> *Identified with:* How much and to what to give is a problem I wrestle with constantly on various levels. I often think of the various biblical references to charity and realize I fall so short and yet I do not feel any easier now about giving freely and completely than I did when I had one-tenth as much as I have now to give. My financial responsibilities have grown ten times, it seems, and of course there is the constant reminder that my physical capacities are on the wane—time is valuable before I become the Lazarus * that you said all of us eventually become. I feel torn both ways and guilty.
>
> On another level there is the problem of how much óf my energy and time I should give my family—even my grown children—to help them and how much I must save to develop myself as a person in my own right.
>
> *Good news* heard and possible *effect:* It is always good news to me to be reminded that my problems are universal, not just mine. The "good effect" upon my thinking is the knowledge that being human—not God—I can never solve them fully. My own personality tends to be the kind that says persevere and you will succeed, and there are really times when that only makes it worse for everyone. It was also very enlightening to see that this was another reason why Christ had to be crucified. He had to become a Lazarus. When I was young, I didn't really see why God made such a drastic climax. It didn't seem like a kind God.

Preaching as Person-to-Person Telling

Person-to-person telling, which is the manner of preaching which this manual encourages, is reported by Berelson and Steiner as the most effective medium for verbal communication:

---

*Lazarus, the beggar, in Luke 16:19-31, one of the Bible lessons on which the sermon was based.

Word-of-mouth or personal communication from an immediate and trusted source is typically more influential than media communication from a remote and trusted source, despite the prestige of the latter.[4]

I corroborated this finding by talking with a random sample of commuter bus riders. I found that 80 percent of the people thought that person-to-person communication had the greatest effect on them. Sadly, only 20 percent had heard preaching which they felt was person-to-person. Too often preaching was felt to be unrealistic platitudes or addressed to everybody in general and no one in particular.

Preaching as person-to-person telling is neither reading a manuscript nor performing a memorized oration. Rather, for me, such preaching is one person, a pastor and friend authorized to speak, after thoughtful preparation, telling a message which speaks to me and which, I hope, will speak to others in the congregation. So, for a sermon to be *telling* is dependent upon both the style of speaking and the result of speaking; for a "telling" sermon means an "effective" sermon, one which effects greater faith, hope, or love.

Preaching as Telling a Story

A corollary to thinking of preaching as person-to-person telling is thinking of preaching as telling a story. This does not mean that all sermons will be narrative. Rather, it means that the sermon will incorporate some of the dynamic of a story and move like a story. A second grade child captured the dynamic of a story by explaining, "'It has to begin . . . and then'—making a quick gesture through the air—'it has to go right along. And something has to happen, and then it has to stop.'"[5]

As with a story, I want a sermon to begin somewhere, to go somewhere, and to have something happen. Usually, the first part of my sermon begins with a description of some aspect of the human dilemma, which I hope is both accurate and empathetic and to which I can respond, "That's me." Then, I affirm some aspect of the gospel which speaks to me in that situation and to which I can respond, "Thank God." What happens is that, to some extent, my mind and heart are carried along in the movement from dilemma to dilemma-resolved-by-gospel. What I hope will happen in the congregation is something like what has happened to me.

To the extent that the sermon "story" is relevant both to our lives and to the gospel of our Lord, it is happening experientially in the minds and hearts of those who participate in the sermon event. Then, the sermon functions as "word" in the biblical sense. It is a happening; it is an act which effects results. As Isaiah says of God's word, "The word that goes from my mouth does not return to me empty, without carrying out my will and succeeding in what it was sent to do" (55:11, JB).

Sermon Story and Biblical Story

I began preparation for this particular sermon with a set of Bible lessons taken from a lectionary. There are a number of lectionaries available which suggest sets of lessons, and some denominations set forth official lectionaries. Some ministers prefer to preach through the Bible, or books of the Bible, in a systematic way. In any case, it is important to use a broad cross section of Scripture each year for preaching in order to preach the fullness of the biblical witness, and it is important to study and reflect on the Bible lesson(s) as the primary source for the sermon.

I read the lessons in a prayerful way, that is, with the expectation that through them God would speak to me. This listening phase of sermon preparation is primary in regard to authority as well as to content. Listening through Scripture for a message which speaks to me and which, in the sermon, I might share, means that I can preach with the authority of a messenger who delivers a message which he has received. Such authority makes no claim for infallibility. Rather, to preach in the name of God says that, as a messenger, I share what I believe I heard God say to me at this time. At the same time, a listener might well say that I must have had a poor connection, and I might well wonder later how I ever thought such a message came from God.

Of course, when I speak of listening for God to speak to me through the lessons, I am not speaking tape-recorder language. Rather, I am speaking of a method of Bible study—a hermeneutic—in which the lessons serve as a kind of transparent, overlay verbal "map" through which to perceive the "territory" of human life and through which to perceive the gospel of Jesus Christ. Thus we are enabled to live in the "territory" authentically.

The two lessons, designated in the lectionary and used for this sermon, were an Epistle lesson, 1 John 4:7-21, and a Gospel lesson, Luke 16:19-31. The Gospel lesson tells the parable of the rich man who refused to help the beggar, Lazarus, and was, therefore, consigned to hellish torment. The Epistle lesson tells of the perfect love of God which casts out fear.

As was outlined in chapter 1, the lessons were approached with questions about their (1) verbal content, (2) structure, and (3) dynamics. Could the content of the lessons be summarized in a Synopsis with the structure and movement of a story? Could the Dynamic Factors which effect the movement be discerned?

In the parable, two of the Dynamic Factors, of which we spoke in chapter 1, are clearly identified. When identified, these factors serve as important clues for further questioning and pondering. They serve as "holy places" on the lesson "map" at which we stand still and listen. The symptomatic behavior is the refusal to share "good things" with Lazarus. The resulting consequence is the torment in Hades. So, on the left-hand (or "sin") side of a sheet of paper, I began a verbal map of the situation in the story which incorporated the rich man's symptomatic action and the resulting consequences:

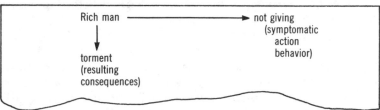

I began to identify, relatively speaking, with the rich man's situation. One might have identified with Lazarus or with the rich man's brothers; but, in comparison with Lazarus, I, and most of us, are rich. Lazaruses cry out to me for help. Our church magazine, the week before the sermon, contained three appeals for money, each with a picture of a starving Lazarus, pleading for help. Our parish has committed us to give toward the relief of hunger. I know the biblical injunctions to give and the threats of judgment for not doing so. Yet I do not give as much as I could, for I have some money saved up which I do not need for current living expenses. Sometimes I feel, as the rich man must have felt, that I wish the Lazaruses would go away and stop looking at me with their pleas for help. But the Lazaruses do not go away, and I could identify with some of the hellish torment of the rich man. There is the pain of conscience and the threat of social upheaval by the Lazaruses of the world.

This symptomatic behavior and resulting consequence comprised the initial human situation in the "territory" of the life story which the Gospel lesson "mapped" for me. But what is the complication that prevents my doing that which I know I should? In what beliefs and perceptions is the symptomatic behavior rooted?

The Epistle lesson provided another dimension to the map by suggesting *fear* as the clue to the root of my sinful behavior. Identifying and elucidating this Dynamic Factor is a critical step toward change in the person and, thereby, in the person's behavior.

John says that fear has torment because fear prevents our loving others. The word *fear* seemed to be a fruitful clue to follow, so I asked, "Of what was I afraid in relation to Lazarus?" I discovered, first, that I am afraid that I might give in the wrong way and be guilty of doing more harm than good. Actually, there is no way to be certain of giving in the right way. On one side, a sociologist, using the model of a lifeboat, argues that, if we in the lifeboat with limited resources keep letting others on board, we will all go under. So, beyond a point, hunger relief is portrayed as immoral. But, on the other hand, our Lord says that as we feed the hungry, we feed Him; and as we do not feed the hungry, we let Him starve (Matthew 25:31-46).

Secondly, and more acutely, I discovered that I am afraid of becoming a Lazarus myself; and I hear a lot of other people express this fear. There can be no certainty of having enough saved up for hard times, and hard times are bound to come.

Thus, the Epistle lesson mapped an obstacle on the territory of life which prevents moving from the place of not giving to the place of giving or, maybe more importantly, to the place of making giving decisions free from bondage to fear. I found the complication in the story to be rooted in this two-pronged fear. So I enlarged my verbal map as follows:

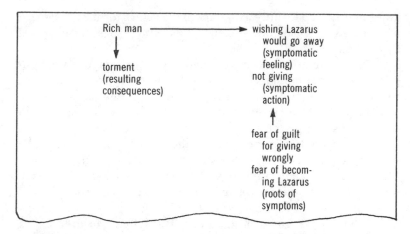

Having mapped a situation and complication with their Dynamic Factors, I sought a resolution. So the next Dynamic Factor to seek would be the gospel content, which might resolve the fear and move me from the "sin-territory" of the left-hand side of the map to the "faith-territory" on the right. What gospel affirmation might transform the rich man into a person who could face Lazarus with compassion and give what seemed right? What gospel might tranform me into a person who could join with Lazarus in the bosom of Abraham?

The Epistle lesson provided another clue, this time to the gospel content. John says that perfect love, that is, the love of God for us, casts out fear; and this love of God for us enables us to love. As I pondered this clue, I began to hear the gospel of the love of God as his mercy, forgiving me and deigning to use my gifts to some good purpose even though I give in the wrong way. In the offertory, we dramatize this gospel. We bring ourselves and our gifts, with all that is wrong about them, in the assurance that God, in his mercy, will accept and use us and our gifts for his good purpose. This gospel alleviates the fear of guilt for giving wrongly.

Furthermore, I began to hear the gospel of the love of God for me as his providential care, providing for me and all his children— not in a utopian way, but, even as we inevitably become Lazaruses in dying and death, God raises us up to his eternal care. In the Lord's Supper, God's providential care for us is dramatized as we gather as his children around his table to receive not only earthly food but also a foretaste of heavenly food. In all worship, God's providential care is dramatized, because God allows us to come into the place which symbolizes his presence on earth for us. This gospel affirmation alleviates the fear of becoming a Lazarus. The gospel content is the Dynamic Factor which changes the root of the symptomatic behavior and, thereby, changes the behavior.

Now I could complete the map of the change which God was producing in the territory of me, through the lessons and the questions which I had pondered:

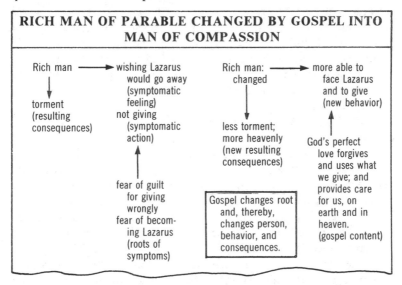

RICH MAN OF PARABLE CHANGED BY GOSPEL INTO MAN OF COMPASSION

In concluding the listening phase of sermon preparation, I recognized that I cannot cast out fear by sheer willpower. I cannot even make myself believe in the gospel of God's love expressed in his mercy and care for me. But, week by week, as I hear this gospel communicated by dramatic actions and by words, it may be so impressed upon my mind and heart that it becomes more operative in my life.

Designing the Sermon

Having, as a listener, received a sermon for me, I then became a messenger whose task is to share what I have received with my sisters and brothers. Therefore, a sermon must be designed so that in about fifteen minutes others may experience something of what I have been pondering for maybe that many hours in bits and pieces over maybe that many days. One of the reasons church folk provide their preachers with livings is so preachers can have time to do this kind of listening to the Lord.

In preaching, I want to share the sermon as person-to-person telling; so I must get a *Synopsis* of the sermon in my head so clearly and simply that I can "see" what I want to say. Maybe, then, the sermon will be clear and simple enough for effective *oral* communication. The importance of telling a sermon first struck me when, after I had read a sermon from five pages of essay-style manuscript, a parishioner poignantly asked me, "Mr. Crum, if you can't remember what you want to say, how do you expect me to remember it?" A clear Synopsis helps both preacher and congregation remember.

The length of the Synopsis is about that of synopses which are printed in theater programs; and, usually, the structure of the sermon synopsis is like that of a play: namely, situation, complication, resolution. The Synopsis has to be clear and simple enough to be remembered easily. It incorporates the Dynamic Factors, and it moves with the flow of a story. It contains the key words which carry the message. The Synopsis summarizes the content which I hope people can remember and reflect on when the sermon is over. It prevents cluttering the sermon with extraneous material.

The Synopsis of the present sermon follows. Note that all the Dynamic Factors which were on the map are incorporated in the Synopsis.

Sermon Synopsis

I. *Situation:* Like the rich man in the Gospel lesson, we are beset with pleas from Lazaruses for help; but, again like the rich man, we wish they would go away, and we refuse to give, in spite of the torment we feel when we refuse;

II. *Complication:* And what prevents us from giving as we should is a two-pronged fear: a fear of guilt for giving wrongly and a fear that, if we give of our resources, we may become Lazaruses ourselves;

III. *Resolution:* However, the Epistle lesson assures us of God's perfect love for us, which casts out fear: a love which forgives us and uses our gifts even though we give wrongly and a love which cares for us, even when we become Lazaruses, and promises us this care into eternal life; and, in the assurance of this love, we can face the Lazaruses and make decisions about giving, free from bondage to fear.

Having synopsized the sermon story I want to tell, I designed an introduction which I hoped would gather the attention of the congregation to the same territory in life which the sermon would map. (See the sermon transcript appended to this chapter.)

Sometimes I write a full manuscript as a means of getting the sermon clearly and simply in mind. Sometimes I tell the sermon out loud several times extemporaneously, maybe to someone else, maybe to a tape recorder.

Then, in preaching, as in a story, I hope something telling will happen by the telling of the sermon, namely, some movement from the human dilemma in sin to life within the gospel. In the sample sermon we have been using, fear makes the demand to give to Lazarus an insolvable dilemma, humanly speaking. If I don't give, I neglect other people; I intensify the torment of conscience; and I contribute to impending torment whether it be world revolution or hellfire. But, if I do give, I exacerbate my fear of guilt for giving in the wrong way and my fear of becoming a Lazarus. Moralistic or idealistic exhortation would worsen the situation. Only an authoritative assurance from beyond the dilemma can resolve the dilemma. This assurance is found in the good news of God's merciful and caring love for us, which enables us to respond to God's holy love. Thus we give or not give in obedience to him, not out of fear of the consequences.

Sermon as Integral to Worship

That the sermon and the Bible are integral to each other has already been demonstrated. In preaching, one way of integrating the worship event is to make this relationship explicit. For example, in this sermon, after an introduction saying that the sermon was about fear and the perfect love which casts out fear, I said that the fear I had in mind was the kind of fear which would prevent the rich man from helping Lazarus in the Gospel lesson.

The sermon can integrate other aspects of worship too. What is said in words in the sermon may be also said in the words or actions of worship. Such connections can be made explicit as in the sermon under discussion.

The concept behind the attempt to integrate other aspects of worship with the sermon pictures worship as a multimedia communication system, through which God addresses us, but which contains so many messages that a worshiper cannot receive and process all of them. When our minds get overloaded with too much rich material, we cannot relate to any of it thoughtfully. But a sermon can highlight certain aspects of worship for attention and thought. To continue the communication system concept, the sermon can, like the mixing panel of a broadcasting studio, mix those aspects which are integral to the one message. These aspects are thus focused onto the mind of the worshiper and attended to in thought. Others of the superabundance of messages in our rites can be left in the background until another time.

Not only can the sermon integrate worship; but, if the gospel is so preached that "peace" happens and people respond with "Thank God," the rituals of shaking hands and giving thanks become genuine experiences and not mere rote. Sadly, such an experience has been so often lacking that the very word "ritual" often connotes meaningless rote.

What Preaching Can Accomplish

I have recounted the development and design of a sermon using the method set forth in the rest of the manual. Now, I want to say a bit about what preaching can accomplish.

With all of us suffering from information *implosions*[6] in which we are battered through the media by more words than we can take in and process and from which we escape by tuning out, it may seem sheer wistfulness to hope that another fifteen minutes of talk can accomplish anything. Yet, week after week, an amazing number of people voluntarily gather for worship, at considerable expense, and most of these people say that the sermon is a very important factor in worship.

In a recent survey, some five thousand clergy and laity of the forty-seven denominations represented in the Association of Theological Schools were asked to rank factors involved in a person's "readiness for ministry." The "cluster" receiving top ranking was "Relating Faith to Modern World," and in this cluster, "Presents the Gospel in terms understandable to the modern mind" ranked first with a mean score of 6.538 out of a possible 7. The second-ranked cluster was "Theocentric-Biblical Ministry," and in this cluster, "Leads worship so it is seen as focusing on God" ranked first with 6.417. "When he is through preaching, you are conscious of Jesus Christ" ranked second with 6.220. Out of 444 readiness factors, "Believes the Gospel she/he preaches" ranked highest with a mean of 6.842 out of 7.[7]

Some time ago *The Virginia Churchman* conducted a "Sermon Poll." Eighty-two percent of the respondents agreed that "Good preaching probably brings modern people to a given church as much as poor preaching keeps them away," and 71 percent of· the respondents agreed that "Some sermons have profoundly influenced my basic outlook on life."

What is there about preaching that warrants such high expectations? Basic to what preaching can accomplish is the interaction of language, perception, and behavior. As suggested earlier, we perceive the territory of life—ourselves, other people, the world—through our verbal maps. We behave according to these perceptions, for they constitute reality for us. In terms of the sermon example I have been using, to the extent that I verbally map and thus perceive myself as having to attain my own rightness by always giving in the right way and to the extent that I verbally map and thus perceive my future as having to insure my own security, to that extent I am prevented from giving to Lazarus. However, to the extent that I map and perceive my rightness as the verdict of the merciful God and my future as given by the providence of the caring God, to that extent I can give or not give to Lazarus without being consumed by fear for myself.

According to the commonsense "wisdom of the world," the former map would be held as the way to life. According to the "foolishness of God," the latter is the way. Yet, as Paul says, God has made foolish the wisdom of the world, and it has pleased God through the foolish message of his preaching to save those who believe. (See 1 Corinthians 1:18-25.) Preaching shares the verbal map of the biblical faith, foolish though it seems according to the wisdom of the world, with the hope that the biblical map may so frame perception and behavior as to be the way to life for the world. Some of the ramifications of this basic hope are as follows:

1. Preaching can help set a healthy tone for parish life. It is true, as has been pointed out, that by sanctioning certain behavior, the parish, as a social system, often teaches with more authority than the preacher.[8] Yet, the preacher, by speaking officially to the people in the congregation, recognizes areas of concern, authorizes certain levels of honesty, and legitimates vocabulary.

2. Preaching can nurture the preacher and the congregation and thereby prevent some of the need for crisis ministry. Dr. Karl Menninger suggests that this can be done:

> Some clergymen prefer pastoral counseling of individuals to the pulpit function. But the latter is a greater opportunity to both heal *and prevent.* . . . Clergymen have a golden opportunity to prevent some of the accumulated misapprehensions, guilt, aggressive action, and other roots of later mental suffering and mental disease.[9]

3. Preaching can draw on the mental and spiritual resources of the whole congregation. My first bishop told me that, as he visited parishes, he could tell in which ones nurturing preaching took place. Where it had not, people sat with heads down, expecting nothing at sermon time. Where it had, people sat with heads up, expectant and attentive at sermon time.

Where there is such participation in the sermon event, preaching becomes a community activity. Facial expressions, body movements, laughs, sighs—all contribute to the event. Beyond the bounds of worship, beyond informal input, preaching draws on congregational resources in pre-sermon Bible study groups, sermon input groups, and sermon feedback groups.

4. Preaching affects the larger society through Christians scattered to their various vocations and ministries in the world. "The daily actions of thousands (or millions) of group members . . . through their continuous participation in political, economic, educational, and kinship institutions" exert a far greater influence

than does the church as an institution.[10] On the basis of his appreciation of the generally unsung role of Christian laity in shaping history, the historian Herbert Butterfield has said, "Those who preached the gospel for the sake of the gospel, leaving the further consequences of their action to providence, have always served the world better than they knew."[11]

Preaching "the gospel for the sake of the gospel" differs sharply from moralistic preaching by which the preacher dictates, harangues, or advises fellow Christians what they should do in their vocations and ministries, although the preacher might not brook the same from the congregation. Whether done by demanding, scolding, or pleading, moralistic preaching persuades no more effectively than other forms of moralistic communication. Can you imagine being persuaded through being scolded by a TV commercial for not buying its product? The point is that our behavior is based on our perceptions; therefore, to change voluntary behavior, perception must be changed.[12] So the commercial tells you the "gospel" of its product—how happy it makes your family or your dog or your friends or you—with the hope that you will decide for yourself that you want to buy it.

The negative results of preaching about social issues in a moralistic way have been evident. Studies have shown that when a communicator, such as a preacher, contradicts another person's "commitments, dedications, and cherished positions in highly involving matters (matters relating to family, sex role, religion, school, politics, or profession)," feelings of "uncertainty or anxiety" will be produced; and the person will denounce the source of the contradiction and try to eliminate it. When commitments and dedications, which are central in a person's life, are attacked, that person feels attacked and, by taking "relentless and persistent, even . . . frantic" measures, sets up a counterattack as the best defense.[13] Have you not observed such response to moralistic preaching?

Although Abraham Lincoln was a person with a profound and biblical sense of his vocation and ministry, he was not appreciated as such by the many preachers who moralistically told him what he should do. To one clerical delegation, President Lincoln replied:

> I am approached with the most opposite opinions and advice, and that by religious men, who are equally certain that they represent the

divine will. . . . I hope it will not be irreverent for me to say that if it is probable that God would reveal his will to others, on a point so connected with my duty, it might be supposed he would reveal it directly to me; for, unless I am more deceived in myself than I often am, it is my earnest desire to know the will of Providence in this matter. *And if I can learn what it is, I will do it!* . . . I must study the plain, physical facts of the case, ascertain what is possible and learn what appears to be wise and right. The subject is difficult, and good men do not agree.

. . . I can assure you that the subject is on my mind, by day and night, more than any other. Whatever shall appear to be God's will I will do. I trust that . . . I have not in any respect injured your feelings.[14]

Summary

In overview, the preaching which we propose entails two major steps. First, as a listener, you listen through the Scripture lessons for an enlightening message, a verbal map, which helps you name and interpret some aspect of the human dilemma, and for an enabling message, a gospel affirmation, which helps resolve the dilemma so you can live in a more fully human way. Second, as a messenger, you share this message with the church gathered for worship in the hope that it will help them, also, to live in a more fully human way as they scatter to their vocations and ministries in the world. For, as Paul wrote, "Faith comes from hearing the message, and the message comes through preaching Christ" (Romans 10:17, TEV).

Appendix: Sermon on the Rich Man and Lazarus based on an Epistle lesson, 1 John 4:7-21, and a Gospel lesson, Luke 16:19-31.

(The sermon was preached extemporaneously without manuscript. Following is a transcript from tape. It is divided into component parts to delineate the structure of the story-like movement.

Dynamic factors are noted in the left-hand margin. Notice that the resulting consequence of "torment," which could have been incorporated in either the situation or complication, was omitted, although I think it was communicated by implication and tone. Sometimes in the complication section the sermon story goes deeper into the root of the situation, as was done in this sermon. At other times, the complication may include the resulting consequences. Or it may do both. The Dynamic Factors can be incorporated into the sermon in many ways, as appropriate to the sermon content. The transcript is typed in an oral format to demonstrate a type of manuscript which allows the preacher who uses a manuscript in the pulpit to come close to extemporaneous telling. Try reading the sermon aloud.)

Introduction
In the Epistle lesson this morning,
    St. John speaks about our FEAR,
and, then,
        he speaks of the PERFECT LOVE OF GOD
            which casts out that fear, to free us from fear.
            The kind of fear that we focus on this morning
                is the fear
                that the Rich Man in the Gospel lesson
                    must have felt.
I. Situation—The Rich Man and Lazarus and Us:
The RICH MAN
    had the beggar, LAZARUS, at his door.
He was there every morning,
    asking to be fed, and asking to be healed.
The Rich Man couldn't face Lazarus,
    and I believe at least one reason
        the Rich Man couldn't face him
    is that he was AFRAID.
            ► I think, if you are like I am,
                you can identify with the Rich Man.
            We are thought of as the rich of this world,
                as Americans, as Episcopalians.
            Anyone, who has a relatively decent house to live in,
                and a good diet,
                is relatively rich,
                    surrounded by a majority of Lazaruses.
            Figures vary, but, somewhere, they say,
                60 percent of the world might be the Lazaruses,
            and the 30-40 percent, to which we belong,
                are the rich men.
            ► And we are constantly bombarded

with the needs of the Lazaruses of this world.
You can hardly open your mail
without getting some request.
Everywhere you turn,
on television, magazines, folders
that come in the mail, there is a starving child,
an emaciated mother, or someone lying sick,
looking up at you, like a Lazarus.

symptomatic ►And, sometimes, there is a kind of feeling
feeling that the Rich Man must have felt in the story:
behavior "I wish it would all go away; I can't face it."

II. Complication—A Twofold Fear:
I can't face the Lazaruses
because I am AFRAID FOR MYSELF.
The fear that possesses us and consumes our energies
and makes it, at least for me and maybe for you,
difficult to face the Lazaruses of the world,
I think is twofold.
The spirit of fear,
I don't think is an individual thing;
it is something that is pervading our thoughts more and more.
►This fear, on the one hand,
is a FEAR OF DOING WRONG.
How shall I use whatever riches I have?
► How much shall I give away?
There are sociologists,
who use the model of the lifeboat:
we've got limited food on this lifeboat,
and, if we let more people on the lifeboat,
finally the whole lifeboat may go down,
and we all end up in the drink.
So there's a very rational and reasonable
sounding argument
which says that,
if we give away anything to feed the hungry
or to relieve poverty,
we're simply exacerbating the problem
rather than solving it.

(Of course, this always assumes
    that we're the ones in the lifeboat,
    and somebody else is outside.)
On the other hand,
    we hear the words of our Lord
        to sell what you have and give to the poor,
    or, inasmuch as we've fed the hungry
        or not fed the hungry,
        we've done it unto him.
So, the choices range
    all the way from giving everything
    to holding on to what we've got.
    How much shall we give, and how do you know?
► And, to <u>what</u> shall we give?
Even in the hunger program,
    which our parish is focused on,
    there is a decision to make
    between world relief and the local program.
And aside from hunger,
    there's the need of the sick,
    and HOPE, and CARE.
And, of course, there's your own family,
    and your own future.

root[1]
       So, one kind of fear is the fear
           of not knowing whether I can do the right thing:
           the fear of GUILT for doing wrong with
               what I have

root[2]
     But, I think there's a much deeper fear:
        the fear that maybe we will become Laza-
        ruses; and,
       if we give too much to Lazarus, we may end
        up a Lazarus.
A man, who is probably wealthier than any of us
    and perhaps you would think is more secure
    and unafraid than any of us in this room,
    was telling me that he went to his pastor recently
    and said he had a problem—
        a problem with his wife.

The problem was this:
His wife was waking up at 2 o'clock in the
    morning,
night after night, crying,
and she was crying about a fear
that he would leave her destitute,
in spite of the fact that they had
several hundred thousand dollars income
and a fine home and good stocks and savings.
But she was in terror and fear
    that he would leave her destitute.
And then he said,
"As I talked, I realized that my wife
was expressing my own fear,
that in spite of all this I'm still afraid.
I'm afraid that I, too, may be (he didn't use
    the word)—
    that I, too, may be a Lazarus."

	This fear can consume us
symptomatic	and keep us from dealing with the problems
action	in the kind of economic and rational way
behavior	that we need to.

III. Resolution—Perfect Love Casts Out Fear:
The Epistle lesson this morning
    speaks of the perfect love, which casts out fear.
I don't have that perfect love, and you don't have it,
    but maybe what we're doing
    as we gather together this morning and Sunday after Sunday
    is to hear of that love of God for us,
    until it begins to soak into us,
    sort of get into the brain cells and our minds and hearts,
    to the point that we begin really to believe it,
    and begin to know it,
    and to that extent, the fear begins to get cast out.
It is not something that we can just do by resolution:
    Tomorrow I'm not going to be afraid any more!
But it is something that happens to us
    as we gather week after week.

►This perfect love of God speaks, first of all,
to the fear of doing wrong.
The perfect love of God says to me
that I never can do *the* right thing,
and you can't do the right thing.
What is the right thing?
To whatever we give,
we're leaving something undone that needs to
be done.
There's no way to do the right thing.
And, yet, God forgives us;
he still accepts us as his children.

*gospel
content*[1]

As in the Confession and Absolution,
he forgives us of our sins,
and, through the Body and Blood of Christ,
he washes us clean and makes us his children
and uses us.
So, whether we give to this or that
or how much we give,
it's as though he gathered up our offerings
and said, "I will make use of what you do;
maybe make use of you
if you give to none of these causes."
This love gives a wonderful freedom
from the kind of fear that possesses and
consumes us,

*new
behavior*

so we can try to deal with our giving
as mature, adult, Christian men and women.
►And, the other aspect of perfect love,
which speaks to me, and I hope to you,
speaks to the fear of being a Lazarus.
Yes, we will eventually all be Lazaruses,
for we will be beggars.
We will be completely helpless, finally, in death.
And, before that, in many ways
we may become Lazaruses—helpless, dependent people.
Our Lord himself, God made flesh,

became a Lazarus on the cross:
    poor, helpless, full of sores.
Yet, he promises, through all of this,
    God still cares. He will not let us go.

gospel
content[2]

    We still belong to him.
The promise of the resurrection,
    the promise of new life in God,
        outweigh all the threats of being a Lazarus.
To believe this perfect love of God in this world
is no easy thing for me.
In fact, if he had not become a Lazarus
    and suffered with us
    and taken the cross upon himself,
I would have a hard time believing
    that he was a good God and a loving God.
But he did.
He shared with us the being a Lazarus,
    and the fear and anxiety on the cross.
    So we can have confidence,
        not only that he forgives us,
            but also, in a way, we can forgive him;
            we can believe that he is a good and loving
            God.
These Bible lessons today ˙
    do not solve the problems
    of how much shall I give;
        or what shall I do with my goods;
            and what shall I do about our hunger
            program?
There's no formula.

new
behavior

But, even as I say this out loud—
        and I hope maybe as I say it out loud to you—
I feel some relaxation of the kind of fear
    which possesses and prevents dealing with
        the thing
    in a kind of rational way.

Conclusion:
So, if you're like the Rich Man and like I am,

often <u>afraid</u> as we face the Lazaruses of this world
and wishing they'd go away,
   and sort of blinded and possessed by fear,
the promise of the love of God,
   the love which, on the one hand,
      <u>does not condemn us</u> whatever we do,
      to give us the freedom to do what seems right,
   and, on the other hand, the love which will <u>not let us go</u>
      and which will finally <u>take care of us,</u>
      even if we should become a Lazarus in the world,
      which we will, finally, in death:
this love of God
      gives us the kind of <u>confidence,</u>
         the kind of <u>freedom from fear.</u>
      that enables us to love.
And I think this is a part of what the Epistle lesson said today:
   that we are able to love others
      because God first loved us.

Chapter 3

TWO MORE
DETAILED EXAMPLES
OF SERMON DEVELOPMENT

*This chapter recounts two examples of sermon develop-
ment in more detail than chapter 2. Again, the process
matters more than the actual sermons. The same process
and the same lessons, used at another time or by another
person, would most likely generate a different sermon.
The reader is encouraged to simulate doing the process
while reading the examples.*

We all function within some framework of thought whether we
are aware of it or not and whether it be biblical-Christian or not.
Thus, we all interpret Scripture within a framework of thought
whether we are aware of it or not, and we design sermons within a
framework of thought. My plea is that we let the framework be
biblical-Christian and that we let it be congruous with sound pastoral
theology and communication theory. The process for preaching
which this manual proposes is intended to facilitate that end.

First Example

The first example is a sermon based on a set of two lessons, one
from the Old and one from the New Testament. The lessons follow:

Isaiah 58:1-12

58 "Cry aloud, spare not,
  lift up your voice like a trumpet;
  declare to my people their transgression,
    to the house of Jacob their sins.
 2 Yet they seek me daily,
    and delight to know my ways,
  as if they were a nation that did righteousness
    and did not forsake the ordinance of their God;
  they ask of me righteous judgments,
    they delight to draw near to God.
 3 'Why have we fasted, and thou seest it not?
  Why have we humbled ourselves, and
    thou takest not knowledge of it?'
  Behold, in the day of your fast you seek your own pleasure,
    and oppress all your workers.
 4 Behold, you fast only to quarrel and to fight
    and to hit with wicked fist.
  Fasting like yours this day
    will not make your voice to be heard on high.
 5 Is such the fast that I choose,
    a day for a man to humble himself?
  Is it to bow down his head like a rush,
    and to spread sackcloth and ashes under him?
  Will you call this a fast,
    and a day acceptable to the Lord?

 6 "Is not this the fast that I choose:
    to loose the bonds of wickedness,
    to undo the thongs of the yoke,
  to let the oppressed go free,
    and to break every yoke?
 7 Is it not to share your bread with the hungry,
    and bring the homeless poor into your house;
  when you see the naked, to cover him,
    and not to hide yourself from your own flesh?

 8 "Then shall your light break forth like the dawn,
    and your healing shall spring up speedily;
  your righteousness shall go before you,
    the glory of the Lord shall be your rear guard.
 9 Then you shall call, and the Lord will answer;
    you shall cry, and he will say, Here I am.

  "If you take away from the midst of you the yoke,

the pointing of the finger, and speaking wickedness,
10 if you pour yourself out for the hungry and satisfy the desire of the
 afflicted,
 then shall your light rise in the darkness
 and your gloom be as the noonday.
11 And the LORD will guide you continually,
 and satisfy your desire with good things,
 and make your bones strong;
and you shall be like a watered garden,
 like a spring of water,
 whose waters fail not.
12 And your ancient ruins shall be rebuilt;
 you shall raise up the foundations of many generations;
you shall be called the repairer of the breach,
 the restorer of streets to dwell in."

Matthew 5:43–6:8.

43 "You have heard that it was said, 'You shall love your neighbor and hate your enemy.' 44 But I say to you, Love your enemies and pray for those who persecute you,45 so that you may be sons of your Father who is in heaven; for he makes his sun rise on the evil and on the good, and sends rain on the just and on the unjust. 46 For if you love those who love you, what reward have you? Do not even the tax collectors do the same? 47 And if you salute only your brethren, what more are you doing than others? Do not even the Gentiles do the same? 48 You, therefore, must be perfect, as your heavenly Father is perfect.

6 "Beware of practicing your piety before men in order to be seen by them; for then you will have no reward from your Father who is in heaven.

2 "Thus, when you give alms, sound no trumpet before you, as the hypocrites do in the synagogues and in the streets, that they may be praised by men. Truly, I say to you, they have their reward. 3 But when you give alms, do not let your left hand know what your right hand is doing, 4 so that your alms may be in secret; and your Father who sees in secret will reward you.

5 "And when you pray, you must not be like the hypocrites; for they love to stand and pray in the synagogues and at the street corners, that they may be seen by men. Truly, I say to you, they have their reward. 6 But when you pray, go into your room and shut the door and pray to your Father who is in secret; and your Father who sees in secret will reward you.

7 "And in praying do not heap up empty phrases as the Gentiles do; for they think that they will be heard for their many words. 8 Do not be like them, for your Father knows what you need before you ask him."

Discerning a Synopsis in the Lessons

Often a set of lessons from the two testaments will complement each other and together offer a complete message, as they did in this example. Note that whereas the Dynamic Factors tended to precede the Synopsis in the Bible study described in chapter 2, in this case the Synopsis precedes the Dynamic Factors. The point is that in either order both can emerge through the Bible study as a complete message with verbal content, story-like structure, and a dynamic.

Reading the lessons, starting with the Old Testament, I was looking for a description of a facet of the human situation in the "then" time of the lesson. The first underline provided clue words for such a description, namely,

> . . . they seek me daily, and delight to know my ways, as if they were a nation that did righteousness and did not forsake the ordinance of their God. . . .

The meaning of this verse was exposited in the *Amplified Bible* with its parenthetical amplifications of the text. This version read,

> . . . they seek . . . and delight [externally] to know My ways; as [if they were in reality] a nation that did righteousness and forsook not the ordinance of their God. . . .

So the lesson described a situation of disparity between the religious practices of the people and their other behavior. Worship was approached seeking one's own way rather than God's way.

The complication, which resulted from this situation, is indicated by the next underline:

> . . . you fast only to quarrel and to fight and to hit with wicked fist . . .

When we seek our several ways, rather than a common way, dissension results.

I read on, hoping there might be some gospel content which might offer a resolution to the situation-complication which was emerging. The third underline in the Isaiah lesson pointed in the direction of gospel: "The LORD will guide you continually, and satisfy your desire with good things. . . ." However, it gave no gospel *content* which might, in fact, satisfy one's desire. I was looking for a gospel affirmation which might authentically satisfy the desire (whatever this root desire was), which causes seeking our own way in contention with others. The word "desire" translates the Hebrew *nephesh* which refers to the essential life of a person. Therefore, the desire in question must be of central importance.

Leaving a question mark by the root desire for the time being, I read into the New Testament lesson. Jesus described the new result which the gospel should effect, namely,

> Love your enemies and pray for those who persecute you. . . .

This behavior would be much happier than the hostility which Isaiah described, but the question remained: what gospel content was there in the lessons to effect such new behavior?

Because of the theology I brought to bear, I questioned the translation in verse 45 which said to act lovingly "so that you may be sons of your Father who is in heaven." This seemed to say that we establish ourselves as children of God by our own good works. So I checked *The Amplified Bible* and it read,

> Love your enemies and pray for those who persecute you, to show that you are the children of your Father Who is in heaven. . . .

Here, loving behavior is depicted as a visible fruit of having already been established as children of God. This translation agreed with the dominant biblical witness, so I tentatively decided to use it as I continued to "listen" through the lessons for a message.

So here is the germinal synopsis I got from the first reading:

SITUATION	COMPLICATION	RESOLUTION
They pretend to delight to know God's ways;	But, actually seeking their own way (in order to satisfy some desire?), they end up quarreling, fighting, and hitting;	However, as a child of God you are enabled to love even those enemies who persecute you.

Note how the lessons furnished the clue words and structure for this germinal synopsis. In map language, the lessons furnished the "places" or topics on which to focus and the relationships between them. The question about the translation of verse 45 was a question of structural relationship on the theological map. Does a person get to being a child of God first and then to loving behavior, or is it the other way around?

Discerning the Dynamic Factors in the Synopsis

The next step was to "listen" through (or "see" through) the clue words and structure of the Synopsis for a sermon to me which I could share with others. It is in this step that the concept of the five Dynamic Factors is especially helpful, for they help the preacher question and understand the human situation-complication which the lesson exposes as well as help the preacher hear the gospel which transforms it.

I will describe this step in the order of Situation, Complication, Resolution, one at a time; but, in practice, the brain may be working on the total sermon story. Also, I am reporting only the most productive steps in the process. Other study of author, date, historical context, etc., provided the ambience for the interpretation.

1. *Situation:* What were the people actually doing then? The point seemed to be that the people went through the *form* of religion (in this case, fasting), pretending to want to know and do the way of God. But what the people really wanted was to maintain their own ways. The RSV reads,

Behold, in the day of your fast you seek your own pleasure . . .

with the alternate translation, which is preferred by the *Interpreter's Bible,*

Behold, in the day of your fast you pursue your own business.

So, while pretending to seek God's way, everyone is seeking his or her own way.

2. *Complication:* Whatever was going on in each person's seeking his or her own way led to the hostilities which I called "hateful conflict." The word for "fight" in the Hebrew lexicon of *Strong's Concordance* (which can be used even by one who does not know Hebrew) was defined as an "argument which totally rejects the other," and "hit" meant "hit to kill." So the conflict was not simply a spat among friends; it was hateful conflict between persons seeking to maintain their own ways of life.

In the complex of the Dynamic Factors, this hateful conflict could be treated as symptomatic behavior on the action level or as resulting consequences on the action level. I treated it as the latter. The task, then, is to follow the clues from hateful conflict to what symptomatic feeling-behavior, based on what root perception, could produce such destructive results. When a person reacts hatefully to someone of another way of life, the person must feel that the other way of life threatens his or her very personhood. In this feeling that one's very personhood is threatened by another way of life, a symptomatic feeling-behavior has emerged. But why? What perception of things underlies the symptom and leads to the hateful results? The *root* of the symptom must be diagnosed if more than exhortation not to feel and act that way is to be preached.

Here the word "desire" serves as a clue word. We desire security of personhood; and, if we try to base this security on our way of life and our way of life is threatened, we feel that our total personhood is threatened, and we react in hateful conflict. This diagnosis rang true for my life and for the lives of people I have known. I could say, "That's me; that's us." [1]

The questions raised by the first three Dynamic Factors had been answered; but, before going on to the resolution of the story, more concrete details were needed for the situation-complication. First, what is meant by "personhood"? Three facets of personhood seemed pertinent: (*a*) rightness of me as a person, (*b*) worth of my actions, and (*c*) confidence of an abiding place for me. Then, an example of conflicting ways of life was needed. I wanted a conflicting pair with which all the congregation might identify. I decided to speak of the *old* way of life and the *new* way of life.

3. *Resolution:* The clue to the gospel content, which might answer the desire for security of personhood, hung only on *The Amplified Bible* translation of Matthew 5:45. The critical word in the Greek is *ginomai (genēsthe)*. Thayer, *Greek-English Lexicon of the New Testament,* gives possible meanings as "to show one's self, prove one's self" and "to be found, shown." [2] In addition, Smith-Goodspeed offers a corroborating translation,

> But I tell you, love your enemies and pray for your persecutors, so that you may *show yourselves* true sons of your Father in heaven. . . . (italics mine)

Thus, the point is not that we make ourselves children of God by our loving behavior but, rather, that loving behavior results from knowing that God has adopted us.

In this affirmation, our personhood is secure. Our rightness as persons is mercifully imputed to us through the cross. Our actions are given worth by God's use of them in his purpose. We have an abiding place for us in God's love. This gospel content speaks to the root of the hateful conflict behavior and enables the new result of loving even those who confront our way of life. For this gospel and for its resulting behavior, I could respond, "Thank God."

Notice that, as the sermon story is developing, you, the preacher, are participating in the story—the movement is happening in your own life. God, through the lessons and the interpretation thereof, is speaking a judging and saving word to you as he did to the people in the Bible and as he will through you to those with whom you share the story. You are not writing a sermon as you might write a notice for the bulletin. You are engaged in a form of prayer with God about an eternal life or death matter.

The Synopsis as Map

The Synopsis, incorporating the Dynamic Factors, laid out as a map for perceiving life territory would now look something like this:

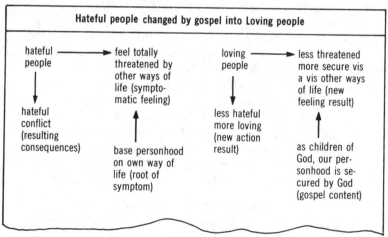

The map may or may not be actually sketched out on paper. The essential thing is to get the clue words and their structural relationships (as discerned in the lessons) clearly in mind and through them perceive life territory. This structure of experience—cognitive, affective, and active—needs to be clearly enough in mind to sketch on paper, whether you actually do it or not.

Dynamic Factors Worksheet

In order to identify what is needed for the movement from being a hateful person to being a loving person to happen, I asked questions which are suggested by the Dynamic Factors. As a help in asking and answering these questions in a manner which is personally relevant, with experiential flow and logical coherence, I developed the Dynamic Factors Worksheet. The worksheet seeks to insure personal relevance by beginning with the subordinate clause, "When we (or I) . . ." It seeks to insure experiential flow by moving as a story. It seeks to insure logical coherence by incorporating all the factors into one sentence, albeit an ungainly sentence which would not be used in the sermon.

As will be explained in more detail in chapter 6, the development of the dynamics of the sermon can begin with any of the five factors, for they comprise an integrated whole in the experience of human change. However, the *symptomatic* action or feeling and the *root* perception are the two factors most often used for starting. Therefore, two worksheet forms are shown in this chapter: one starting with the *symptom* and one starting with the *root*. A sample of the Dynamic Factors Worksheet beginning with the *symptom* follows. It is filled out as it was in preparing this sermon. (A sample worksheet, beginning with the *root,* will be included in the second example of sermon development.)

DYNAMIC FACTORS WORKSHEET
stating the Dynamic Factors of the sermon
in one sentence, starting with the *symptom.*

When we are   *feeling TOTALLY THREATENED as persons when*
        (SYMPTOMATIC BEHAVIOR in feeling and/or
        action, described in nontheological, commonly familiar
        language.)
our way of life is confronted by a different WAY OF LIFE,

because   *we base our PERSONHOOD—our rightness as persons,*
(ROOT perception which underlies the Symptomatic
Behavior, described in nontheological, commonly
familiar language.)
the worth of our actions, and our confidence about a continuing place
for us—on our particular way of life,

and which results in *HATEFUL CONFLICT against persons in*
(RESULTS in action, if not included above, and
consequences, described in nontheological, commonly
familiar language.)
different ways of life by forming cliques of like-minded persons, by
being hypercritical of those who are different, and by squeezing out
those who threaten us,
God says to us   *"You do not need to base your personhood on your*
(GOSPEL content which speaks good news to root.)
way of life, because you can base it on being a CHILD OF GOD, in
which your Rightness is given through the Cross; the worth of your
actions is given in that God deigns to make use of them; and you can
be confident about a continuing place for you because God has the
future and you in his hands,"
which   *reduces the feeling of total threat to us by other*
(NEW RESULTS of Gospel in behavior and consequences, described in nontheological, commonly familiar
language.)
ways of life, so we do not need to resort to hateful conflict, but, from
the security of personhood based on being children of God, we can
appreciate as well as criticize other ways of life and we can criticize as
well as appreciate our own ways of life.

The Sermon Synopsis

The process so far has been primarily that of the preacher listening for a message for himself. The preacher could say, "That's me," to the people in the Old Testament lesson who reacted to another way of life with hate. Through personal reflection, using clue words in the lesson, the preacher identified a cause of this hate as being threatened by other ways of life and identified the root of this threat as basing one's personhood on one's way of life. Then the New Testament lesson affirmation that as children of God our essential personhood cannot be threatened spoke as gospel, which evoked a "Thank God" and could result in a more loving response to other ways of life.

Now the preacher's role shifts from listener to messenger. How can the experience, which the preacher gained through the lessons, be experienced by the congregation through a sermon? To do this, a sermon needs to be designed which tells a story which incorporates the Dynamic Factors which moved the preacher. To achieve such a design requires a Sermon Synopsis something like the one which follows. A Synopsis not only summarizes the sermon story as a whole but summarizes each of the sections. Such a Synopsis enables the preacher to unfold the sermon through progressive stages of experience. If a manuscript is written, a Synopsis worked out before writing saves much time and facilitates clarity. Whether a manuscript is written or not, a Synopsis provides a handy outline for preaching extemporaneously.

Try reading the following Synopsis aloud. As brief as it is, does it not tell a complete story that involves your life?

Sermon Synopsis
(with Dynamic Factors noted)

INTRODUCTION: Sermon based on lessons—about
    (1) our differing ways of life
    (2) hateful conflict between differing ways of life
    (3) possibility of love in spite of differing ways of life

  I. SITUATION: We each seek a congenial way of life, but our ways of life differ;

 II. COMPLICATION: And, when we base our total personhood (that is, our rightness as persons, the worth of what we do, and confidence about a | *root* continuing place-for-us) on our congenial way of life, and our way of life is confronted and we feel <u>threatened</u> by another way of life,

symptom

we try to protect our way of life, and this self-protection leads to <u>hateful conflict;</u>

result

III. RESOLUTION: However, in the Gospel lesson, Christ not only <u>commands</u> love between differing ways of life

but also <u>enables</u> love by <u>reducing the threat of</u> other ways of life to us

by telling us that, as <u>children of God,</u>
(*a*) by the cross we are right as persons;
(*b*) what we do is given the highest worth because we are used by our Father; and
(*c*) in our Father's hands we have confidence about a continuing place-for-us;

gospel content

so we can oppose other ways of life <u>without hateful conflict,</u> and we can admit wrongs in our ways of life as well as
share our ways of life with others, that is, we can be <u>more loving.</u>

new result

The Sermon Manuscript

The sermon was preached from a manuscript which looked much like the following, except there were more open spaces and underlinings. The manuscript is abbreviated by omitting secondary words from sentences and merely noting examples. Such a manuscript can be used as an outline for carefully planned extemporaneous preaching. Try "preaching" the sermon aloud, filling in where the manuscript is abbreviated.

<u>Introduction:</u> Sermon based on lessons:
about (1) our DIFFERING ways of life
(2) HATEFUL CONFLICT between differing ways
(3) possibility of LOVE in spite of
differing ways of life

I. Situation—Differing Ways of Life:
► First, our differing ways of life:

   ► OT lesson: Isaiah spoke to people,
        OSTENSIBLY seeking GOD'S way of life,
        but, actually, seeking CONGENIAL way,
        i.e., seeking way which suited them.
   ► So, WE, if you are like me,
       seek CONGENIAL way of life,
       a way suitable to OUR tastes and values.
   ► BUT, ways of life congenial to us DIFFER.
     e.g., Two ways: OLD and NEW
     As I describe them,
       see which most congenial to you.
     Afterwards, show of hands.

   ► OLD emphasizes:
       (*a*) DUTY—duty to God, country, organization
          e.g., R. E. Lee on "duty"
       (*b*) SELF-CONTROL—not show feelings
          e.g., Emerson on "self-control"
       (*c*) FUTURE—forego NOW satisfaction for future
          save money for future
          abstain from sex until future
          wait until older
 ► NEW emphasizes:
       (*a*) SPONTANEITY—do own thing
          trust feelings and act on them
          "if it feels good, do it"
          "duty" = four-letter word
       (*b*) SELF-EXPRESSION—let it all hang out
          be open, honest, confrontational
       (*c*) NOW—now generation
          why wait? do it now
          may not be future; live <u>now</u>

 ► Which most congenial to you? Hold up your hand.
     Old? New? Some of both? Nothing so far?

 ► So, right here in this congregation

our congenial ways-of-life DIFFER.

II. Complication—Hateful Conflict When Personhood Threatened:
► Now, differing ways of life become CRITICAL PROBLEM
   when lead to HATEFUL CONFLICT.
   ► HATEFUL CONFLICT in lessons:
      FIGHTING with intent to destroy
      ARGUMENTS which totally reject other person
      HATRED of other person as enemy
   ► OR, Hateful Conflict in OUR lives:
      Hateful Conflict between parents and children
         between husband and wife
      Hateful Conflict between Democrat and Republican
         between liberal and conservative
      Hateful Conflict between high church and low church
         old way and new way
   ► HOW does Hateful Conflict
      between differing ways of life COME ABOUT?
      ► Hateful Conflict takes root
         when we base our LIVES—our TOTAL
         PERSONHOOD—
         on a PARTICULAR, CONGENIAL WAY OF LIFE.
      EXAMPLES of basing total personhood on way of life:
         —When base RIGHTNESS-AS-PERSON on particular
            way of life,
            desperately need to PROTECT the way of life
            which CONFIRMS Rightness-as-person.
         —When base WORTH-OF-THINGS-YOU-DO
            on particular way of life,
            desperately need to PROTECT the way of life
            which ACCEPTS and APPROVES things you do.
         —When base CONFIDENCE ABOUT CONTINUING-
            PLACE-FOR-US
            on particular way of life,
            desperately need to PROTECT the way of life
            in which we have a PLACE.
   ► THEN, to the extent we base Total Personhood,
      that is, Rightness-as-person

Worth-of-things-we-do
Confidence about continuing-place-for-us,
to the extent we base Total Personhood
on OUR way of life,
to that extent, when our congenial way of life
is CONFRONTED and THREATENED
by DIFFERENT way of life,
we feel TOTALLY and ULTIMATELY threatened as
TOTAL PERSON.
► AND, when feel TOTALLY THREATENED, if want to LIVE,
only choice is to PROTECT YOURSELF,
and this SELF-PROTECTION leads to HATEFUL
CONFLICT.
EXAMPLES of Hateful Conflict:
—To protect Rightness-as-person, form CLIQUES
to confirm each other's opinions and beliefs.
Leads to Hateful Conflict with other cliques,
name calling, slurs, exclusion.
—To protect Worth-of-what-we-do
become HYPERCRITICAL of what others do.
By CONDEMNING and DEMEANING,
lower worth of what OTHERS do,
so relatively raise worth of what we do.
Leads to Hateful Conflict in backbiting and gossip.
—To protect Continuing-place-for-you
SQUEEZE OUT others who threaten your place.
Leads to Hateful Conflict for INCLUSION.

IN SUMMARY, to extent we base our Total Personhood
—rightness-as-persons
—worth-of-actions
—confidence about continuing-place-for-us
on OUR OWN way of life,
other ways of life will so TOTALLY THREATEN us
that we can only react
in SELF-PROTECTIVE, HATEFUL CONFLICT.
In this condition,
LOVE between differing ways of life is IMPOSSIBLE.

III. Resolution—Loving Response When Personhood Secure in Gospel:

►YET, in NT lesson, Jesus commanded such LOVE:
  "Love your enemies and pray for those who persecute you
  to show that you are children of your Father in heaven."
►BUT, how can you LOVE someone
  who threatens your very personhood?
    your rightness-as-a-person?
    the worth-of-what-you-do?
    your confidence of a continuing-place-for-you?
►I cannot love someone who is a total threat to me.
►You cannot love someone who is a total threat to you.
►HOWEVER, the marvelous thing is
      that the word which God speaks to us in NT lesson
      that we are children of God our Father—
  this word REDUCES the level of threats.
  When we know that we are children of God,
    our personhood is secure in God
    and we are less threatened by different ways of life.
  EXAMPLES:
  —As children of God our Father,
    by God, by the cross, we are RIGHTED-as-Persons.
  By the cross, we know God is ALL RIGHT God:
    he suffers WITH us, to share what he does to us;
    he suffers FOR us, to pay penalty for our wrongness.
  And God GIVES US this RIGHTNESS.
    By cross he says that you and I are RIGHT-as-persons.
    By the Body and Blood of Christ, we are made right.
  Christ and His Body and Blood
    are made present for us as we gather for
      Holy Communion.
  We are made right in God's eyes,
    and you can't be any righter
    than to be right by God.
  —As children of God our Father,
    by God, what-we-do is WORTHED.
  God, in his PATIENT MERCY,
    USES our actions in his purpose.

Even our MISTAKES, even our IMMORAL actions,
    God uses to teach us, to test us,
        to punish us, to bring us to him.
  As God mercifully accepts and uses our offerings
    of money, of bread and wine, of prayers and praise;
    so he uses us and all that we do.
  And, when GOD uses something,
    that gives it the HIGHEST WORTH.
  By God's patient, merciful use of what-we-do,
    we are assured of the WORTH of our actions.
—As children of God our Father,
    in the long run, when all is said and done,
    we can be CONFIDENT of a CONTINUING-PLACE-
    FOR-US
      in his care, in his hands.
NOTHING, not even getting squeezed out of this place,
    or getting squeezed out of this world in death,
  nothing can take away our place
    in the loving care of God.
    In the Holy Communion, we pray
      that he may dwell in us and we in him.
    There is a Continuing-Place-for-Us
    in the Hands of God.
► SO, as children of God,
    we are secure, by God, in our Personhood:
    secure in Rightness-as-persons;
    secure in Worth-of-what-we-do;
    secure in Continuing-place-for-us.
  As children of God,
    our Personhood is secure
    because it is based on GOD and his love for us.
► SO, as children of God, secure in our Father,
    we don't need to PROTECT ourselves, our personhood,
    by Hateful Conflict.
  As children of God, secure in our Father,
    even when we OPPOSE different ways of life,
    we can do so without Hateful Conflict.
► AND, as children of God, secure in our Father,

we can ADMIT the WRONGS of OUR OWN way of life, and

we can SHARE our ways of life with others in a little more loving way.

Second Example

The reader may prefer to skip this example for now and either try using the process to develop a sermon or read on into the rest of the manual.

The lesson for this sermon was Ephesians 5:15-24, in the King James Version.

> See then that ye walk circumspectly, not as fools, but as wise, redeeming the time, because the days are evil. Wherefore be ye not unwise, but understanding what the will of the Lord is. And be not drunk with wine, wherein is excess; but be filled with the Spirit; speaking to yourselves in psalms and hymns and spiritual songs, singing and making melody in your heart to the Lord; giving thanks always for all things unto God and the Father in the name of our Lord Jesus Christ; submitting yourselves one to another in the fear of God.

The "Then" Situation and Complication

Looking at the "then" situation historically, the Epistle to the Ephesians was written about A.D. 60, probably by Paul, as a general letter. In the cultural context of the letter, most people believed that events were controlled by Fate, which was in turn controlled by the Stars. Therefore, there was an atmosphere of pessimistic resignation because of this belief that the events of life were dealt out by an arbitrary and impersonal power. In such a belief, what people did counted for nothing.[3]

Looking at the epistle theologically, on the one hand, Paul described the grand sweep of the mystery of God's purpose for the human race, namely, to make all people "members of the household of God," and heirs of "the love of Christ" and "the fullness of God." But, on the other hand, the letter describes the incongruous behavior of Christian people. Members of the "household of God" were still practicing sexual immorality and filthy talk. Christian people, to whom the "love of Christ" had been proclaimed, were still selfish and covetous. People, who had received "the fullness of God," were still being taken in by Gnostic anti-material spirituality. So Paul might easily have felt that his labors were for nothing, and the people might have felt that their practice of religion was for nothing.

This belief, or suspicion, that human activity might be *for nothing* appeared as a salient factor in the "then" situation. But did the lesson touch that theme?

Clue Words and Map

It was not clear, from the translation, what Paul was saying, so I began exegeting the lesson by underlining words which struck me as clue words to follow up for a message. (See the underlined words in the Bible passage.) Other words could have emerged as apparent clues and might do so at other times.

These clue words seemed to form a germinal story line, the first sketchings of a map. The clue words and their structural relationships looked something like this:

SITUATION	COMPLICATION	RESOLUTION
The "days are evil";	So (by implication, at least) we do not make melody in our hearts but rather get drunk with wine;	However, when we "walk circumspectly. . . , redeeming the time. . . , understanding what the will of the Lord is," we make melody in our hearts to the Lord.

These words of the lesson were given. But to what in life territory were they clues? What territory did they map? To follow the clues, the Greek text and Thayer's *Lexicon (Grimm)* were used, beginning with the phrase "the days are evil."

Exegetical Study of Clue Words

I found that the word "evil" *(ponēros)* can mean evil in the sense of being "pressed and harassed by labors," which are evil in the sense of being "expressive of unintermitted toil and carrying no suggestion of results."[4] And I found that the word "days" *(hēmera)* can mean the chronological "duration and length also of human life."[5] So a situation began to emerge to which I could respond, "That's me"— the relentless dailiness of one day after another, pressured and harassed by unremitted toil, often with no suggestion of results. In a word, a picture of drudgery. In addition to addressing my life, the lesson also seemed to be addressing the *for nothing* experience of the original audience. The distance between the "then" and the "now" was closing.

From the evil days of drudgery, Paul says that we can "redeem the time." The word "time" (*kairos*) often means *purposeful* time, the time of "opportunity to do something."[6] Purposeful time, time for *something* and not for nothing, can be redeemed from the drudgery of "unintermitted toil . . . carrying no suggestion of results." The word "redeem" *(exagorazō)* can mean "to make a wise and sacred use of every opportunity for doing good so that zeal and well-doing are as it were the purchase money by which we make time our own."[7]

So more story began to emerge, namely, redeeming time by taking time from the purposeless drudgery of the dailiness of unremitted toil and spending the time for a fulfilling purpose.

This raised the question, for what purpose? So, using the word "circumspectly" *(akribōs)* as a clue, I found that its meaning includes "deviating in no respect from the law of *duty*."[8] Here was an intimated resolution for the story in the purpose of devotion to duty.

But duty to whom or to what? This question is answered when Paul speaks of "understanding what the will of the Lord is," in which "will" *(thelēma)* means "what one wishes or has determined shall be done,"[9] and in which "understanding" *(suniēmie)* means "to put (as it were) the perception with the thing perceived; to set or join together in the mind, *i.e.,* to understand."[10]

Here, then, is the theological promise which fills the emptiness of drudgery for nothing. When what you perceive as the will of the Lord is joined together in your mind with what you do, the duration of life is redeemed from drudgery to purposeful time. Your life is used by God.

Dynamic Factors Worksheet

Through the exegesis, the Dynamic Factors, which effect the movement from the old way of "walking" to the new, begin to work. The clue words in the structural movement of the lesson begin to interpret and affect the preacher's life. They begin to map the preacher's territory and to move the preacher from the old place of drudgery, in thinking that life is like being assigned to hard labor with "no suggestion of results," to making melody in the assurance that God uses our labors for his good results.

In order to get the Dynamic Factors in this movement into coherent order and sharper focus, the Dynamic Factors Worksheet provides a useful tool. Because I had begun with the perception that often life appears to be for nothing as in the myth of Sisyphus,[11] I used the worksheet beginning with the root perception. The worksheet beginning with the symptom would have done just as well. This is how the worksheet shaped up:

DYNAMIC FACTORS WORKSHEET
stating the Dynamic Factors of the sermon
in one sentence, starting with the *root.*
When we think/believe   *that our lives are hard labor with*
(ROOT perception which underlies the Symptomatic Behavior, described in nontheological, commonly familiar language.)
no anticipation of results,

which issues in   *feeling that life is drudgery and that we*
(SYMPTOMATIC BEHAVIOR in feeling and/or action, described in nontheological, commonly familiar language.)
are drudges so that in our actions we work without heart or
get drunk to endure the drudgery or hate those who drudge us,

and which results in   *not being able to live [as the Epistle*
(RESULTS in action, if not included above, and consequences, described in nontheological, commonly familiar language.)
says] singing and making melody in our hearts to the Lord.

God says to us,   *"You are on duty for me; I am with you in*
(GOSPEL content which speaks good news to root.)
your daily life; I use what you do to effect my good results,"

which issues in   *our being able to put our hearts into our*
(NEW RESULTS of Gospel in behavior and conse-

quences, described in nontheological, commonly familiar language.)

work; we don't need to get drunk; we don't need to hate those who make demands on us; and we can thank the Lord for occasions to serve him.

Synopsis of the Sermon

After further reflection on life territory through the enriched lesson map and recalling examples in his own life, the preacher works out the Synopsis of a sermon story by which the congregation might share an experience similar to the preacher's experience with the lesson. The Synopsis which follows incorporates the biblical clue words and the Dynamic Factors. No manuscript was written and the sermon was preached extemporaneously, using the Synopsis as an outline. Again, try reading the Synopsis aloud. Even in its brevity, does it not tell a story which is the story of many people and maybe yours?

Sermon Synopsis

INTRODUCTION: In the lesson, Paul says to us
  (1) "See that you walk circumspectly . . . , understanding what the will of the Lord is,
  (2) Redeeming the time,
  (3) Because the days are evil."
In the sermon I will
  (1) Describe the <u>drudgery</u> of life when "the days are evil," and
  (2) How the time of our lives can be <u>redeemed from drudgery</u> by walking circumspectly . . . , understanding what the will of the Lord is.
  I. SITUATION: First, describe life in which "the days are evil":
     If you are like I am, you can identify with Paul's statement that the days are evil, in which <u>days</u> refers to the mechanical, by the clock, routine, dailiness of life, and in which <u>evil</u> means evil in the sense of being <u>assigned to hard labor with no anticipation of results.</u>
       e.g., the myth of Sisyphus
       e.g., taking care of your own person

e.g., working at home, at school, on the job

II. COMPLICATION: Now, if you are like Sisyphus, assigned to hard labor with no anticipation of results, life feels like drudgery and you feel like a drudge; *symptom*

then you go about life and work without putting your heart into it, for you can't put your heart into drudgery,

so you may, as Paul says, get drunk to endure the drudgery, or you may begin to hate those who drudge you, e.g., family, teacher, boss, even yourself, or life, or God. *result*

(At least, when life and work feel like drudgery, and your heart is not in it,
you can't go about, as the Epistle said,
"singing and making melody in your heart to the Lord.")

III. RESOLUTION: So the question is how can the time of our lives be redeemed from the drudgery?
Paul says, "Walk circumspectly . . . , understanding what the will of the Lord is," which means living as a person on duty for the Lord, the Lord who is with us, who uses us to effect his good results: *gospel*
    e.g., Brother Lawrence
    e.g., offer up life and work to the Lord
so even Sisyphus work is not drudgery when it is work for the Lord;
    we can put our hearts into our life and work,
        don't need to get drunk to endure,
        don't hate those who assign work to us;
    rather, when our lives are redeemed from drudgery
        as we live for our Lord,
    as Paul says, we can give thanks for every occasion
        to serve our Lord,
    for this is what life is for. *new result*

Chapter 4

BIBLICAL INTERPRETATION FOR PREACHING

In this chapter, hermeneutical doctrines and hermeneutical process, which have been alluded to or implied in the examples of sermon development, are stated more explicitly and systematically.

The preacher who begins with the Bible begins with a document written in another age, in another language, to another people, in another culture. If the sermon is to be related to Scripture, the preacher cannot avoid hermeneutical issues. That is, the preacher cannot avoid being a "Hermes" who carries the message from the "then and there" to the "here and now."

Hermeneutical Issues

A generation ago, hermeneutical issues were seldom discussed, at least not by title. The issues of biblical criticism consumed the energy of biblical scholarship. Today, hermeneutical issues are in the forefront and are the focus of sharp debate. There is hardly a biblical, theological, historical, or homiletical issue which has not been designated as a *hermeneutical* issue:

How does religious language function? What is the relationship between language and faith? Is theological language prose, poetry, or parable? Is the truth of Scripture narrative or propositional? Should we do structural or contextual analysis? Do we seek distance from or communion with the text? Are we after truth, insight, or understanding—about self (anthropological)? About God (theological)? Do we question the text or does the text question us? Do we interpret the text or does the text interpret us? Is the experience cognitive or affective? Is the language denotative or connotative? Is the trick to bring Scripture to the modern mind, or the modern mind to Scripture, or to get them apart? Is the text transparent, translucent, or opaque? Does it provide meaning in itself or through itself? Is its message existential or eschatological? Does the preacher seek a literal or a spiritual meaning—allegorical, tropological, or anagogical, analogical, typological, or none of the above? What is the name of this enterprise anyway? Is it hermeneutics, or hermeneutic, or should it be *hermeneutik*?

Every week, even as the debates continue, the preacher must be a hermeneut. Every week, even as hermeneutical issues remain unresolved, the preacher must do the hermeneutical task. The preacher does not ignore the debates. He may learn from them. She may contribute to them. But the preacher cannot chase after every new idea, and the preacher cannot wait until all the answers are in. Therefore, while recognizing the immensity of the hermeneutical issues and the debates about them, this manual makes bold to offer some hermeneutical doctrines, a hermeneutical process, and a hermeneutical model, all of which follow.

Some Hermeneutical Doctrines

Following are the central doctrines which underlie the hermeneutical process. You might want to formulate your own for comparison.

Bible, Preaching, and Preacher

The *Bible,* as the authoritative witness to God's revelatory acts through Israel, leading up to his definitive revelatory acts in Jesus Christ, contains all things necessary to salvation. Therefore, the Bible serves to frame the structure of our preaching and to designate the content.

Preaching is an integral and central function of the church and more especially of the ordained ministry. The commission to preach the gospel is written large in almost all ordination rites. It is commanded by our Lord, "Go into all the world and preach the gospel to the whole creation" (Mark 16:15, RSV), and reinforced by Paul when he asks, ". . . how can they believe if they have not heard the message? And how can they hear if the message is not proclaimed? And how can the message be proclaimed if the messengers are not sent out?" (Romans 10:14-15, TEV).

The *preacher* functions as a listener to God through the Bible before he or she serves as a messenger of God through the sermon. As Gustaf Wingren so aptly puts it, the preacher

> only needs to look honestly within and see how the Word strikes him, how it wounds and upsets him, how he is healed and consoled and restored by it. It is by no means certain that his experience will be shared by his congregation. He is not in the pulpit to turn out his inside but to give voice to the Word. Since he is a man, however, and since all to whom he speaks are also men, he can often let the passage say to them what it has said to him. . . .[1]

Thus the act of a sermon preparation is throughout a form of prayer and involves the preacher on the most personal level, just as listening to a sermon is a form of prayer and involves the listener on the most personal level.

A Doctrine of Persons

The manual presupposes a doctrine of persons which recognizes our state of original sin in which, without some transformation, we would

1. absolutize our perceptions,
2. demand that life obey *our* terms, and
3. establish ourselves permanently in this world.[2]

Our doctrine of persons also recognizes our bondage to original sin until we have been set free by the gospel. In the functional terms of this manual, we are in bondage to whatever word-perception-behavior complex by which we are living until we have been grasped by a new word-perception-behavior complex which is more viable. (See chapter 6 for a fuller discussion of this complex.)

Such a doctrine of persons, by recognizing our bondage,

precludes moralistic preaching. Rather, it demands that the sermon include empathetic description of some facet of bondage to "sin" word-perception-behavior and affirmation of a relevant facet of "faith" word-perception-behavior through which the bondage may be broken and change may be effected.

A Doctrine of God

Our process presupposes a doctrine of God which includes God's wrath in the deleterious consequences of our "sin" word-perception-behavior complexes and which includes God's blessing in the beneficent consequences of "faith" word-perception-behavior.

This doctrine of God includes God's justifying, transforming, and enabling act in Jesus Christ, made present in the preaching of the gospel so that

1. in faith in God's mercy we need not absolutize our perceptions,
2. in loving obedience to the demands of God's providence we need not demand life on our own terms, and
3. in hope in God's abiding presence we need not seek to establish ourselves permanently in this world.

Such a doctrine of God would preclude antinomian preaching and would demand an affirmation of the gospel which would transform not only feelings and attitudes but also transform overt behavior. In a word, such preaching would see justification-sanctification as an integrated event.

A Doctrine of the Word of God

Our process presupposes a doctrine of the Word which includes an awareness of the human being as one who perceives reality through the framework of language and who acts on the basis of this perception; hence the word-perception-behavior complex. Such a doctrine of the Word includes a recognition of the power of language to reframe perceptions and thus to transform behavior.

Lastly, this doctrine of the Word understands the Word of God as God's action in making his *impress* on us, as those who are stamped or marked with characteristics of God. The Word comes to us in this form through the communication event of worship, including both verbal and nonverbal channels. In this total communication event, the sermon is the integrating factor.

A Doctrine of the Holy Spirit of God

Our process presupposes a doctrine of God the Holy Spirit who proceeds from God the Father through God the Son, the Word.

This doctrine of the Holy Spirit includes a recognition that all persons live in and act out of some spirit, that is, some "atmosphere" of existence, some attitude, whether it be the Holy Spirit or some unholy spirit.

This doctrine of the Holy Spirit also recognizes that all gospel preaching is pentecostal preaching; for as God the Word acts upon us through the preached words, so God the Holy Spirit acts upon us, for the Word and the Holy Spirit are inseparable in union with the Father in the one triune God.

A Hermeneutical Process

Both advocates of the older hermeneutics and the newer hermeneutic agree that the hermeneutical task is essential for preaching.

From the older perspective, Bernard L. Ramm forcefully states the importance of hermeneutics for preaching:

> Whether preaching is textual or topical or expository it rests ultimately upon the minister's interpretation of the Word of God. That theological discipline which takes as its goal the proper interpretation of Scripture is hermeneutics. A solid hermeneutics is the root of all good exegesis and exegesis is the foundation of all truly Biblical preaching.[3]

And, from the newer perspective, Robert W. Funk asserts that the role of hermeneut is essential to the ministerial vocation:

> The hermeneut—the one who practices hermeneutic—is he who, having been addressed by the word of God and having heard, is enabled to speak, interpret, or translate what he has heard into the human vernacular so that its power is transmitted through speech. If the minister is not a hermeneut, he has missed his vocation.[4]

In the manual, we are assuming a knowledge of exegetical tools, so we will concentrate on *doing* the biblical interpretation in a way that will facilitate our being spoken to and moved by the lessons as prerequisite for preaching.

Our approach to biblical interpretation is governed by our

hermeneutical doctrines, but the matter of interpretation is language; and, as we have seen, words act upon us to frame our *perceptions (i.e., beliefs, understandings, and attitudes)* and thus language designates our feeling and action *behavior.* Therefore, in biblical interpretation, as the language of Scripture acts upon us, we are also being interpreted. The Word of God, through the medium of language, acts upon us in judgment and mercy even as we do interpretation.

However, we are not acted upon as passive recipients. On the contrary, we approach the lesson(s) with an operational hermeneutics, even if it is unarticulated. That is, we cannot approach Scripture with an empty mind. Rather, we approach Scripture with our memories, our mind sets, our questions, and our needs. A large part of one's operational hermeneutics is often unarticulated and unexamined. But, unless we articulate and examine our operational hermeneutics, we tend to absolutize our understandings of the text as if we had unmediated, direct, infallible communication with God through Scripture. In this section, we are trying to articulate and examine a hermeneutical process, whose structure not only parallels the structure of sermon design but also the structure of the overall plot of the biblical story.

Biblical Situation-Complication

In this hermeneutical process, first, we seek to understand the concrete situation described in the lesson or in the context in which the lesson occurs. Since in this fallen world all human situations are mucked up with sin, the situation will always be a complicated situation. Thus, we shall seek to understand the concrete biblical situation in all of its complication.

The biblical situation-complication will include people—people who feel and act on the basis of some underlying way of wording and perceiving their world. These symptomatic feelings and actions are followed by resulting consequences.

Since the overall thrust of Scripture is God's saving action to restore a fallen world to right relationship with him and thus to transform his people into faithful and obedient children, we shall focus on an aspect of the situation-complication that might be subject to change through preaching. (There will be some *givens* in the situation-complication which are not subject to change through preaching. These elements are not addressed in the sermon.) Focusing more closely on "sin" aspects of the situation-complication, the "sin" feeling of the people in the lesson may be thought of as the *symptom* of the aspect of sin which will be treated in our lives as God speaks to us through the lessons and, later, in the sermon, as the symptom to be treated through preaching. Or we may think of the symptom as the "sin" manifest in both feeling and the action. The essential thing is to stay in touch with the real dynamics of human behavior.

Then, the preacher will seek to understand some of the underlying cause of the situation-complication as rooted in the heart and mind. That is, we seek the *root* which underlies the symptomatic behavior and which may be changed by God's Word speaking through the Bible and through preaching. This root in the heart and mind of the people in the lesson(s) will be their underlying way of wording and perceiving their situation. In the case of "sin" behavior, it will be a "sin" way of wording and perceiving. In theological terms, the root can be thought of as an aspect of the sin condition which underlies symptomatic sins.[5]

The "sin" behavior, which is rooted in the human heart and mind, is followed by some *result*. The result may be thought of as human action and its consequences; or, if the action has already been incorporated into the story, the result may be thought of as only the consequences, consequences both in the life of the protagonist and in the lives of others.

Since the consequences follow "sin" behavior, the consequences will be less than blessed or even positively painful. In theological terms, the consequences may be thought of as God's loving wrath, bringing people to desire transformation. God uses three mediums for his wrath, namely, social, physical, and psychical.[6]

Present Situation-Complication

In the dialogue between the *then* of the Bible and the *now* of our lives, a dialogue which closes the gap and renders the Bible contemporary, an analogous concrete situation-complication begins to emerge in our own lives. Often the biblical words will bring aspects of our history into awareness, and often our experiences will help us understand the life meaning of the biblical words.

Understanding the text involves understanding ourselves in the situation-complication under focus. Therefore, as we seek to understand the symptom (feeling and/or action) of the people in the lesson, and the root, and the result, we are also seeking to understand these factors in our own lives. This aspect of biblical interpretation is emphasized by the "new hermeneutic." This autobiographical aspect of biblical interpretation will be threatening and even painful at times. But it is in this intimate, prayerful dialogue with God through the text that the preacher is renewed and a sermon is born.

Biblical Gospel Resolution

Just as God spoke to the people in the biblical situation-complication, God's Word is ultimately gospel to those who are enabled to believe. In some cases, the gospel may speak an immediate affirmation of God's love. In other cases, the gospel may speak a long-term affirmation of hope in God's sovereignty. But, in any case, the next factor we seek in the lessons is the *gospel content,* which speaks to the root of behavior to effect a transformation in mind and heart.

The gospel content may not be stated in the particular lessons being used; and, if not, the preacher's quest extends beyond the particular lessons to the wider biblical context. Gospel content is what God affirms to us as good news for our transformation. Gospel content is not law (imperative) or conditional affirmation (subjunctive). Rather, gospel content is affirmative promise (indicative) in which God is the affirmer and we are the recipients. It is the effective power of God working through the gospel content, speaking to the root of behavior, which provides the resolution to the situation-complication in the Bible study and, later, in the sermon.

To the extent that the gospel content speaks to the root of behavior with effective power, to that extent those who hear are transformed in heart and mind (*i.e.,* in word-perception) and will feel and act differently. That is, a *new result* will take place which contrasts with the old result. In theological terms, the new result might be called sanctification or the "work of faith."

This new result is not a new imperative added to the sermon as a kind of final exhortation or new ideal. Rather, the new result is a description of the result which, in fact, emerges from having experienced the lessons up to this point. The new result simply continues the story of the Bible study experience a bit further. The doing of the imperative, which was at least implicit in the situation-complication, is made possible by the transformation effected by the gospel of God.[7]

The hermeneutical process we are describing has the structure and dynamics of a story. Something has happened to us in the Bible study: the word has acted; movement and change have occurred; the biblical story has drawn us in and interpreted our lives.

Present Gospel Resolution

As with the situation-complication, we are in conversation with the text in the resolution area of the story. Our previous life in Christ illumines the biblical words, and the biblical words call to remembrance and engender anew the gospel for us.

It may be that the God who spoke to the people in the lessons will speak in a different idiom to us. Since the gospel content speaks to the root of behavior, the idiom of the gospel content should correspond to the idiom of the root. Therefore, in order to be faithful to the text as a medium of God's living Word to us, we may be required to translate the biblical idiom in our interpretation and preaching. For example, a preacher who described living under the weight of sin as trying to swim with a piano on one's back would describe the gospel as God's lifting the piano. Such translation is admittedly a risky and audacious enterprise, but it is necessary if Scripture is to be a living word.

Function of Theology

As we do our hermeneutical work, we will bring to bear our creedal theology, that is, the theology which we actually believe, as well as our insights into ourselves and other people, our knowledge of literature, history, the social sciences, and other aspects of the human situation. What we bring to the lesson(s) can serve to illustrate the content of Scripture, but what we bring also stands under the judgment of Scripture, and this judgment may hurt.

Not only will we bring assumptions and knowledge of which we are aware, but also we will bring implicit assumptions and tacit knowledge of which we are not aware. The calling into awareness and articulation of assumptions and knowledge and bringing them under the test of Scripture are critical aspects of the hermeneutical process, and they provoke uneasiness and pain as well as growth.

Schema of Process

The hermeneutical process described above can be schematized as follows. The order of thought process in practice may correspond to the order of our description, or it may be quite different. The point is that the process forms an integrated whole and it may take place in any order as long as the whole process occurs.

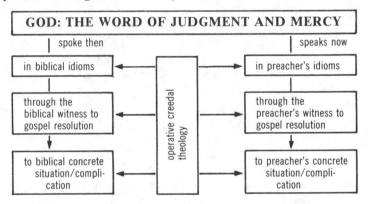

Note that doing this hermeneutical process requires, first and foremost, careful and thoughtful reading of the lessons. What words are there; what is the author saying; what is God saying to us? This initial engagement with the lessons can be tested and enriched by exegesis, using several translations and if possible the Hebrew and/or Greek texts, dictionaries of the Bible, lexicons, commentaries, word studies, and the various types of biblical criticism and analysis. The hermeneutical process described here can help us order the information which exegesis renders and can prevent the accumulation of pages of incoherent notes without a message.

Note, also, that in the hermeneutical process we have delineated the Dynamic Factors, namely, symptom, root, result, gospel content, and new result. In biblical interpretation, the Dynamic Factors make up the underlying dynamics of the story of the people in the lessons and of our experience in studying the lessons. In preaching, they

provide the underlying dynamics of the sermon. The Dynamic
Factors are happening whenever dynamic Bible study and preaching
are taking place. Awareness of them simply reminds us of questions
that need to be asked and areas that need to be explored.

Note also that in the process we have delineated the three
segments of a dramatic story, a story in which something happens,
namely, Situation, Complication, and Resolution, or compacted,
Situation-Complication and Resolution. Sentence summaries of
these segments of the sermon story, connected with conjunctions,
comprise what we have called the Synopsis. In biblical interpretation,
the Synopsis serves to gather the content of the lesson(s) into one
experiential story for the preacher. In preaching, the Synopsis serves
to communicate the content of the sermon with experiential, as well
as logical, continuity.

A Hermeneutical Model

In describing the hermeneutical process, we have spoken of
being interpreted by the lesson and being drawn into the story. But,
the reader might well ask how such metaphors function in practice.
By what model can we conceive of the words of a Bible reading
"interpreting" our lives or of our being "drawn into" a story? By what
model can we conceive of words, and our verbal behavior, affecting
the rest of our behavior? If the hermeneutical field abounds with
unresolved issues, its cognate fields of linguistics and semantics
abound even more. But, again, the preacher cannot postpone
preaching until all the answers are in; so this manual offers the "map-
territory" model as a functional concept of what goes on when we do
biblical interpretation.

The Biblical Passage as Map

In the field of biblical interpretation there are many hermeneutical models. Bible passages are approached as language events,
literature, metaphors, extended metaphors, images, myths, symbols,
dogmas, allegory, poetry, literal prose, moral teaching, and story.
Bible passages are thought of as windows or doors, transparent,
translucent, or opaque, as illustrators, illuminators, guides, sources
of existential insight, presenters of reality, mirrors, inspirers of piety,
keys to life, and food for the soul. I offer "map" as a hermeneutical

model because I have found it simple, functional, and capable of encompassing other models. However, the manual's interpretive process can be done whether this particular conceptual model commends itself or not.

In this model, the relation of language (for example, a Bible reading) to that which is not language is conceived as analogous to the relation between a map and a territory.[8] More precisely, the map is conceived as an overlay map through which the territory is "seen" and experienced, for language frames our experiences.[9]

The map resides in our brains and is composed of what we know, or think we know. As signals from the territory impinge on us, we use our language as an overlay map to ignore some signals and attend to others by awareness, naming, and making sense.

The linguistic overlay map through which we experience and make sense of the territory is also amended by the signals which impinge on us from the territory. Thus, we are engaged in an interaction between our map and the territory which confronts us. Using biblical imagery, the "word," which is the operative map in us at any given moment, "creates" the territory in our perception. The territory as we perceive it through our map is the territory which is "real" for us at any given moment. But the biblical God reveals himself through the objectivity of the territory as well as the subjectivity of our maps. So when our maps do not provide a viable perception of the territory, we seek to replace or amend them. We seek maps that provide a way to fullness of life.[10]

Our maps are diverse and complex. They include the tongues we speak with their various grammars and, in these tongues, the many roles which language plays. However, our present concern is primarily with the maps which Scripture provides, which include factual narratives, myths, legend, poetry, hymns, letters, parables, philosophy, and wise sayings. We will be concerned with these maps as they enable us so to experience and make sense of the territory of our lives that we can live more fully the authentic life for which God made us.

Integrity of Map

The biblical passage as overlay map is not completely transparent.[11] If it were, it would contribute nothing to our perception of the territory. Rather, the map, with its *places* and their *relationships* to each other and its *movement* from one place to another, possesses its own integrity. The content of the map in itself is opaque, and a person can read and ponder the map aesthetically, without seeing through the map. But pondering an overlay map in itself (then the map would be functioning as territory being pondered through another map) does not exhaust its potential function. A person may also see territory through the map; or, more accurately, territory may appear to a person through the map and it appears differently through different maps.[12]

Integrity of the Territory

The territory also has its own integrity, independent of the map. For example, the biblical God of concrete history is who he is and will be what he will be, independent of being named by Moses or anyone else. (See Exodus 3:13-14.) However, no one has a completely open sensorium for perceiving territory because our sensoriums admit some inputs and exclude others according to the map which is operative in us at the time, whether we are aware of that map or not.

The Map Designates Behavior

We not only experience and perceive the territory of life through our maps; but also, because we behave on the basis of our perceptions of ourselves, others, values, etc., the maps which are operative in us designate our behavior. So the adequacy of our maps for finding our ways into life is crucial for survival.

Adequacy of Map

To be adequate, a map, in itself, must offer at least such aesthetic appeal and personal relevance that a person is enticed to ponder and enjoy it.

In addition, an adequate map will permit viewing territory from different perspectives. These perspectives might be described by the various "-logies," such as psycho-logy, socio-logy, anthropo-logy, or theo-logy. These various perspectives need not exclude one another. Rather, they complement each other for fullness of perception. The more perspectives a map provides, the fuller the perception it offers and the greater will be its authority and longevity.

Not only will an adequate map offer a variety of perspectives, but it will also communicate the three-dimensional "whole message" of a hologram. The maps which Scripture contains have the characteristics of a hologram.

When a laser beam illuminates a hologram negative, the territory can be seen in depth and height. This is so because, when the photograph was made, the plate received two beams. A "coherent beam" was reflected from the territory onto the plate. This beam, by itself, could provide multi-perspective information about *places* and their *relationships*. But such a map would lack the vertical dimension of depth and height. In experiential terms, the map would display the dimensions and perspectives of the "-logies" of science. But it would lack glimpses into the mystery of the deeper than human knowledge.

The hologram map reveals a whole, three-dimensional perception because another beam impresses itself on the photographic plate. This beam is called the "reference beam," and it comes directly from the light source. It adds no new information about the territory. Neither does it obscure the information which the "coherent beam" conveys. Rather, when the "reference beam" joins the "coherent beam," it gives the map its third dimension of depth and height. The "reference beam" in itself is invisible; yet it enriches human perception with the vertical dimension of marvel and mystery. Of such quality are the maps in Scripture.

Maps Which Transform

When a map is read, not only with the intent of gaining information and insight but also for personal maturation in Christ, the reader must seek himself in both the map and the territory. One kind of *place* the reader must be able to find himself will be the tragic—the dark and negative places of affliction and sorrow. Another kind of *place* will be the comic—the light and positive places of benevolence and happiness. In human experience there is oscillation between the tragic and the comic. But maturation in Christ goes beyond these dimensions to the third-dimension "mapped" by the Christian faith story. In this dimension, the tragic is perceived as glimpses of crucified life and the comic as glimpses of the resurrected, and the two cannot be dissociated. In the faith story, the way to the place of comedy always includes the way of the cross. Yet the way of the cross always goes beyond tragedy into the comic place of resurrection life.

As we are grasped by the biblical three-dimensional, faith story "maps," we are transformed in "territorial" perception and behavior toward greater maturity in Christ.

Summary

Returning to the *doing* of biblical interpretation, this chapter concludes with a summary of the hermeneutical process for use as a practical guide:

1. We approach the given lessons with the expectation that through them we will be given some fresh understanding of ourselves and some fresh understanding of the gospel of God in relation to ourselves. To accomplish this, we think of the lessons as transparent, overlay maps through which we may perceive the territory of our lives in a fresh way.

2. This approach to the lesson map implies a method of Bible study.

   a. We attend to *clue words* in the lessons as place names on which to focus, both in the text and in our lives. This involves careful reading of the lessons and use of lexicons, dictionaries, and theological word studies.

   b. We attend to the *structure and movement* of the lessons, whether the form is propositional or narrative, to understand relationships in the text and corollary relationships in our lives. This involves entering into what is happening in the lesson and maybe translating and paraphrasing it in a way which exhibits the structure and movement.

   c. We attend to the *then* concrete situation of the lesson to seek to understand its meaning as a map for the life territory of those who first heard it. In this way the Scripture stands before us in its own integrity to help us understand ourselves afresh as we perceive our territory through the transparency of the biblical map. If we do not attend to the lesson in its separateness from us, something like another person, we use it as a mirror to reflect back the old understandings we bring to it and miss out on the new insights it has to offer.

d. We attend to the *now* concrete situation of our lives as perceived through the lesson map, looking for places and relationships in the territory of our lives which are analogous to those in the *then* situation. This stage of the process is usually the most painful as well as the most gratifying. It requires pondering the area of life which the lessons map and pondering it with personal involvement.

3. The structure and movement of the lessons, and the experience of them in the Bible study, designate the structure-and-movement of the sermon; and the content of the life territory perceived through the biblical map designates the content of the sermon. Therefore, the sermon event is a compressed recapitulation of the Bible study event, designed for effective telling for the purpose of drawing those who hear it into the event along with the preacher.

In this process, we try to work out what we want to share in our sermon simply enough that we can *tell* it, person to person, without reading it, as a story which unfolds with experiential continuity and with clarity of content.

Chapter 5

SYNOPSIS OF THE SERMON

This chapter further develops the concept of the Synopsis as a means for achieving clarity, coherence, and movement in preaching. It also elucidates the design of the sermon as story.

If the message of the sermon is to be like the biblical *word,* it will act upon the hearer to effect a movement in mind and heart. Preaching will be an event, a happening. The summary of such a message will be more like the synopsis of a play or story than like the points of an essay about a topic. A "topic" means a place. A sermon which simply makes two or three points about a topic stays in the same place. For example, a sermon can make three points about the topic of hope without going anywhere, with no movement. However, when a sermon is like a story, it will begin with consideration of inadequate hope and move to a gospel proclamation of an adequate hope in God. The hearer would not merely have learned more *about* hope but would have been personally moved to a more adequate hope. Working out a sermon Synopsis contributes to the composition of such a sermon, a sermon which reflects the movement which the preacher experienced in the preparatory Bible study and which can enable the listener to share that experience.

Marks of the Synopsis

A Synopsis summarizes the verbal content of the sermon in two or three segments, in their order of presentation, usually either as

1. Situation-Complication	OR	1. Situation
2. Resolution		2. Complication
		3. Resolution

Sermon Segments Summarized

In the Synopsis each segment of the sermon is summarized in a *complete sentence*. It is important that a complete sentence, not a subject only, be formulated, because it is the predicate which is said about the subject that gives the sermon substance. It is easy to think of subjects. Predicates are more difficult. Complete sentence summaries of the segments of the sermon insure that both subject and predicate receive full consideration. These complete sentence summaries make the "points" of the segments of the sermon.

A complete sentence which summarizes all the content in each segment insures *verbal clarity* in the sermon. In preparing the sermon, material which cannot be summarized in the Synopsis is discarded as irrelevant to the sermon. Until a Synopsis of the sermon is written, the preacher has no basis for making decisions about what ideas to include or leave out as the sermon is being prepared. In delivering the sermon, unless the preacher states the points boldly and explicitly, the listener remains in doubt about the point of what the preacher is saying. Therefore, a well-formulated Synopsis enhances clarity for both the preacher and the listener.

There are two fears which militate against clarity in preaching. One fear is the fear of publicly committing oneself to an idea. If the preacher makes a point clearly, without hiding it under a basket of subtlety, ambiguity, or obfuscation, he or she is exposed and committed. The listener knows what is said and what is meant and can hold the preacher accountable. Deliverance from the fear of human judgment which hinders clarity in preaching requires a faith in God's judgment like Paul's: "With me it is a very small thing that I should be judged by you or by any human court. I do not even judge myself. . . . It is the Lord who judges me" (1 Corinthians 4:3-4, RSV).

The other fear which militates against clarity is the fear of insulting the intelligence of the listeners by being too simple. This may be possible, but in the responses of listeners to hundreds of sermons, I have never heard criticism for being too clear or too simple—too simplistic, yes; but never too simple. On the contrary, confusion about content is the most prevalent criticism. As one responder said, "I want to spend my energy *thinking about* what you are saying, not trying to *figure out* what you are saying." If lack of clarity compels the listener to concentrate on figuring out what, if any, point the preacher is making, reflection on the meaning of the sermon for one's life is prevented.

Not only does a Synopsis with its points in complete sentences expedite clarity by enabling the preacher to state points succinctly and explicitly, the Synopsis also provides the *clue words* which carry the sermon's line of thought. For example, a sermon whose theme is hope might move from the clue words "fragile hope" based on human accomplishments to the clue words "confident hope" based on God's sovereignty.

Words which I am calling "clue words" are often called "key words." The image of *key* words is useful, for such words are like keystones in an arch, or they are like keys to unlock thoughts. However, I prefer the term *clue* words because the image of a clue conveys more of the dynamic function of language. Words can serve as clues which lead a person to remember concrete experience and as clues for holding experiences together in memory. The word "clue" means literally "a ball of thread." With focus on the *thread* image, a clue word means a word which, followed and pondered, will lead to concrete experiences. With focus on the *ball* image, a clue word means a word which makes sense of multifarious experiences by gathering them around one word.

In sermon preparation, a clue word, tenaciously followed, often leads to experiential truth which is relevant to the preacher and, because what is most personal is usually most general, relevant to others also. But, rather than concentrating on a few words as clues, the tendency is to proliferate words from commentaries, from one's verbal storehouse, or from the latest homiletical "aid," superficially, without following any word into the "territory" of experience. Words used superficially function as screens rather than as clues.

However, if like Moses in reverence before the burning bush we will honor a few clue words as holy ground and take off our shoes and stand still and listen, it may be that we will discover the real sermon to which they lead. In reverence we can ask to what concrete experience a clue word leads and follow that clue until we can describe an example in our lives.

After deciding on the clue words to be used in the Synopsis, these clue words are used throughout the sermon. They form the headlines of the introduction. They are used to introduce and relate illustrations. They are central to summaries and transitions.

It is difficult to use clue words too often in a sermon. A sermon on the subject of being enabled by the power of the gospel to preach the gospel to human needs used the clue word "need" (or "needs") eighty-six times and "gospel" sixty-six times. Written responses to the sermon included "excellent continuity," "I always knew where you were," and "continuity from beginning to end." No one suggested that clue words were overused, and no one said anything negative about clarity or simplicity.

As the preacher uses clue words as map places to get to concrete territory, so must the listener as the sermon is being preached. By using only a few clue words and by dwelling on them, the preacher allows the listener time to follow the clues to his or her own life and to use these clue words to tie experiences together and make sense of them. Making points explicitly and using the clue words throughout the sermon are necessary for effective communication of the message. Otherwise listeners complain: "I heard lots of words, but I didn't get the point"; "I heard him talking but I don't know what he said"; or "There were too many words and too many ideas for me to handle in one sermon."

Synopsis Sentence for Coherence

The two or three points in the Synopsis of a coherent sermon can be joined with conjunctions into a Synopsis sentence which summarizes the whole sermon and tells a complete story. The "places" of focus and their relationships, which the sermon maps, are incorporated into the Synopsis sentence. The full sermon merely zooms in on the places and their relationships for more descriptive detail.

Writing a sermon Synopsis that forms one coherent, albeit long,

Synopsis sentence serves both to facilitate and to test the coherence of the sermon. Coherence is essential for effective preaching. Lack of coherence evokes responses, such as "I got lost," "The sermon didn't follow," or "The preacher seemed to jump from one thing to another."

The purpose of the Synopsis sentence is similar to the purpose of what has been called the Sermon Proposition or Subject sentence. However, these latter have tended to be so abstract as to lose the narrative quality and so static as to lose the dynamic of movement. The Synopsis Sentence, while longer, captures both the narrative and dynamic qualities of story. The Synopsis, stated in one, long, coherent sentence, contains what the preacher or listener might say to the inquirer who wanted a three-minute digest of the sermon.

Synopsis and Order of Presentation

The Synopsis of a sermon which has movement will begin somewhere in human experience and will go somewhere. When the Synopsis moves like a story, an experiential flow, a story line, will be built into the order of presentation.

The specific order of presentation which is used in the Synopsis and thus in the sermon depends upon how the preacher thinks he or she can most effectively tell the sermon so that listeners can share what he or she received through the preparatory Bible study and reflection.

Generally, the sermon begins with an introduction to call listener attention to the primary area of concern. The first point will most often describe some facet of the human situation (usually the symptom, or maybe the root or result, or even the gospel content or the new result) with which the listeners can best identify. Then the sermon moves to the Complication (usually the root and/or the result). The Resolution (gospel content and new result, maybe reiterated if used earlier) usually comes last.

Communication theory endorses this order of presentation. There is evidence that an introduction aids retention, for a number of experiments "have all found significant improvement in retention when some sort of introduction was used to focus audience attention on certain parts of the message." There is also evidence that "the safest procedure for the persuader appears to be to put the problem before the solution."[1] Thus, in general, the Situation/Complication precedes the Resolution.

The Dynamic Factors are incorporated into the Synopsis to facilitate movement. Unless the order of presentation moves experientially, listeners complain that "nothing happens" in the sermon. Written responses to sermons that lack movement say: "The sermon went around in circles"; "The preacher had a good idea but he didn't go anywhere with it"; or "It was more like a lecture than a sermon."

Points and Turning Points

There is a tendency for sermons (like any discourse) to manifest the sameness of a flat surface or a straight line and therefore lack interest because conflict, uncertainty, and suspense are lacking. Or, in the sameness of a sermon, the preacher may lose the listener because there are no salient features to mark the way the sermon is going. So a sermon needs not only points, but also, like a story, it needs turning points which identify different levels of feeling and different directions of thought.

The turning points of a sermon might be thought of as the curtains between the acts of a play. The curtains between the acts define distinct segments of the play and prevent sameness. After each act, the attentive viewer summarizes what has happened and waits expectantly for the new direction of the story.

In preaching, the turning points are often called transitions. A transition may be simply the conjunction used to connect the points of the Synopsis into the Synopsis Sentence. For example, in the situation, the preacher may have been describing our Lord's demand that we forgive those who abuse us. Then as transition, she or he may simply say, "But," so emphatically that it stands out as a turning point to the complication of the resentment with which we too often respond to those who abuse us.

More often, a transition-turning point will require more words. Usually a summary of the point of the previous segment is needed, or maybe a summary of everything that has gone before. Then, the next segment is introduced by giving a hint as to what will follow—only a hint for the suspense must not be lost.

Transition-turning points, which summarize what has happened and hint at the new direction in which the story will go, prevent sameness in a sermon. Therefore, (a) transitions form the salient features which enable the listener to "see" where the sermon story is going and to follow it; and (b) transitions distinguish the "acts" of the sermon, each with its own mood. These distinctions provide diversity and interest in the verbal content of the sermon; but, just as important, by emphasizing the turning point, the preacher experiences the mood personally and communicates it with voice and body action. A carefully developed Synopsis can enable the preacher to know the point of each segment, to sense its mood, and to ascertain and feel the turning points.

The role of transition-turning points in preventing sameness in a sermon might be schematized as follows. The circles symbolize the turning points which help the listener follow by summarizing the story and which provide uncertainty and suspense as they hint at where the story is going.

SITUATION: don't yet know the complication; so story is calm.

COMPLICATION: know the complication; so the story is stormy.

RESOLUTION: still know the complication but also know the gospel; so the story is calm in a transformed way.

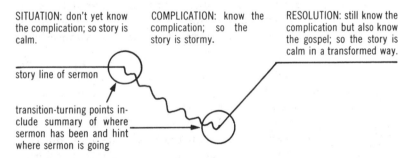

story line of sermon

transition-turning points include summary of where sermon has been and hint where sermon is going

For the believer, interest in a sermon can hardly be achieved by uncertainty over the resolution because one assumes the victory of the gospel will be manifest. But there are other levels of interest. One is the suspense over what aspect of the gospel will be proclaimed and in what images and metaphors it will be expressed. For example, the complication of a particular sermon was a description of how hard it is to maintain a Christian life-style when one is afraid of being laughed at by one's friends. It was certain that the resolution would be something about God's support, but no one knew it would be that "Jesus says to us, 'I am your friend and I don't laugh at you.'"

Another source of interest is in the reassuring reiteration of a familiar story. Human anxiety is rooted in the tacit, if not explicit, awareness of a cosmic battle between evil chaos and good order. So, every week, dozens of TV programs are based on the plot of possible victory by evil, resolved by eventual victory by good, and millions of viewers are reassured that good wins out.

Intellectually the viewers know the resolution in advance. The interest resides in experiencing the reassuring resolution afresh as the familiar story unfolds. Sermons can offer a similar interest.

Synopsis and the Sermon Remembered

Our biblical heritage makes us aware of the critical role of remembering. And we are aware of the effective role of story in bringing to remembrance. A synopsis of a story enables one to remember the full story. Therefore, a story which has a clear and succinct synopsis, emphasizing its points and turning points, is remembered.

The way the synopsis of a play functions closely parallels the way the synopsis of a sermon functions. Suppose you went to see *Detective Story,* and before the curtain you read the synopsis in the playbill:

> *Act One:* In a police station, Detective McLeod reveals his harsh concept of justice by beating a professional abortionist accused of performing an illegal abortion.
> *Act Two:* But, McLeod's harsh concept of justice is shattered when his wife confesses that she once used the abortionist.
> *Act Three:* However, McLeod finds a new concept of justice tempered with mercy and admits the error of his harsh ways, forgives his wife, and prays for pardon.

The synopsis is clear and succinct, but you would probably forget it if you left before seeing the play. However, the concrete and emotional experience of the whole play would implant the synopsis into your brain cells with power. So, after having seen the whole play, you will remember the synopsis; and the remembered synopsis will call to mind the full story.

The importance of story in remembering has been experimentally documented.[2] In the experiment, subjects were presented a "story" composed of individual sentences as follows:

(Sentence 1) The rock rolled down the mountain.
(Sentence 2) The breeze is warm.
(Sentence 3) The rock crushed the hut.
(Sentence 4) The ants ate jelly.
(Sentence 5) The hut is at the river.
(Sentence 6) The story is in the newspaper.
(Sentence 7) The hut is tiny.
(Sentence 8) The jelly is sweet.

Sentences 1, 3, 5, and 7 contain material for the story. Sentences 2, 4, 6, and 8 were interspersed as extraneous material.

Five minutes after the sentences were presented, the subjects were asked which of the following sentences they had seen in the presentation:

(Test 1) The hut is at the river.
(Test 2) The rock crushed the tiny hut.
(Test 3) The rock crushed the tiny hut at the river.
(Test 4) The rock which rolled down the mountain crushed the tiny hut at the river.

Subjects overwhelmingly chose Test 4, with Test 3 coming next. Subjects usually denied having heard Test 2 and Test 1, the only test sentence actually presented in the original series.

From the sentences presented, subjects had abstracted a coherent story and had discarded the extraneous material. They remembered the story, not as four discrete sentences, but as a continuous synopsis. This experiment gives a clue to the way a sermon is heard and remembered.

If a sermon contains material extraneous to the Synopsis, the listener must process and discard it. If the sermon contains only material relevant to the Synopsis but in fragmented form, the listener must piece together a coherent story. If the listener's energy is consumed doing this sorting out and piecing together, remembering and pondering the sermon are impeded. But, if the sermon communicates its Synopsis well, the listener can receive and remember it and still attend to interpreting the sermon for his or her life.

Anytime a preacher is tempted to use bits of material which are not germane to the sermon Synopsis, this experiment might serve as a warning.

Points and Concreteness

The points of the sermon Synopsis need to be general enough to summarize all material in the sermon segment covered by the point. The points also need to be general enough to apply to many people. Yet for a sermon to touch and move people on the levels of feeling and faith, a sermon needs to be concrete. In order to achieve both the verbal clarity of general points and the experiential clarity of concrete illustration, a sermon must move between the higher levels of abstraction in its general points which make up the Synopsis and the lower levels of abstraction in the concrete material which illustrates the points. So, as the sermon story moves horizontally from situation to complication to resolution, it also moves vertically between general points and concrete illustration.

We practice this vertical movement naturally in normal conversation. For example, a person might state a point like, "I had a good time yesterday." The point is verbally clear, but it is so general that what is meant concretely by "a good time" is unknown. Therefore, after such a general point there is a transition to concrete illustration: (a) if the listener indicates a desire to know what is meant by "a good time" and (b) if the speaker wants the listener to know. The transition may be simply a brief pause or the listener may say, "Tell me about it"; or, if interest is shown, the speaker may say, "Let me tell you about it." Then, after concretely describing what is meant by "a good time," the speaker might repeat the general point, "So I really had a good time yesterday."

This vertical movement between general points and concrete illustration, which we do naturally in normal conversation, is often omitted from sermons in three ways. First, the sermon stays on the level of general, highly abstract points and lacks concreteness. So people respond, "I heard the words but it did not touch my life." Or, secondly, the sermon stays on the concrete level, but the points being made are unclear. So people remember examples, but they miss the point. Thirdly, a sermon might have both general points and concrete illustrations but the connections between them are not clear. The connections may be unclear either because the preacher jumps from points to illustration without introducing the material as illustrative of a point or because the preacher does not use the clue words of points in telling illustrative material.

As an example of the vertical movement in a sermon, recall the sermon appended to chapter 2. The complication segment began with the point "I can't face the Lazaruses because I am afraid for myself." The rest of the complication concretized this one point. The fear was delineated as twofold: fear of doing wrong and fear of becoming a Lazarus. Then this twofold fear was illustrated by description and by narrative example. Illustration of a point may be done by concrete *description* of the phenomenon to which the point refers. Or illustration may be done by *example.* Examples may be from literature, firsthand observation, or from the preacher's own experience. If the example is from literature or observation, care should be taken that it is well known as well as familiar to the preacher. If the example is autobiographical, care should be taken that it illustrates the general *point* and not the preacher. In this way an autobiographical example can be made personal to the whole congregation.

In summary, a sermon moves horizontally from beginning to end, from point to point, from situation to complication to resolution. If a sermon also moves vertically from the higher abstractions of explicitly stated general points to the lower abstractions of vividly described concrete illustration and the two are connected, the sermon will be clear. The sermon will be clear on both the verbal map level and on the experiential territory level.

Story, Scripture, and Sermon

Our emphasis on the sermon as story is grounded on (1) what Stephen Crites has called "The Narrative Quality of Experience,"[3] (2) the predominance of story in Scripture, and, therefore, (3) the inherent appropriateness of story for preaching the gospel relevantly to human experience. Let's take a look at these three underpinnings.

Experience as Story

There is a provocative device for getting a small group engaged in sharing personal experiences of life and faith. Each person is given paper and crayon and asked to draw his or her "spiritual (or religious) life line." The line is not to depict external events but is to express one's inner spiritual or religious experiences in relation to external events. The line may move up or down, backward or forward, in circles or zigzags, or in any way expressive of the person's spiritual experiences.

Then, each person tells the meaning of her or his line. What is shared is a person's story, roughly chronological, which is made up of substories, episodes of special significance. Although the stories are told in roughly chronological order, they are not merely chronicles of events. Rather the accounts are stories in that they include conflict and suspense. The conflicts, often precipitated by external events, center in the inner person. Could I endure the strain of caring for the person who needed me? Could I keep trying when failure seemed inevitable? Could I do what I believed was right in spite of disapproval by other people? Suspense is aroused not only because the outcome is uncertain but also because a great deal is at stake in what the outcome turns out to be.

Like these personal stories, all significant experience has the quality of story. Experience flows with a basic chronological progression. But significant experience requires more than a chronicle to map it. A verbal map of significant experience contains the elements of story—conflict, complications, and suspense. Something of value is at stake and the resolution is uncertain, at least humanly speaking. (Is this not the way we relate significant experiences in our lives?)

Scripture as Story

The story character of Scripture was underlined when G. Ernest Wright subtitled his monograph on the *God Who Acts* as *Biblical Theology as Recital.* This recital is telling the story of God's acting in historical events and in individual lives.[4]

This awareness of the recital of story as the chief medium for the revelation of God informed T. O. Wedel's memorable lectures on *The Drama of the Bible.* Dr. Wedel began by pointing out that "all human beings always have lived, do now and always will live, by some kind of story, some kind of plot, some kind of drama in which they know themselves to be actors on a stage."[5] Then Dr. Wedel told the biblical "love story" as the story by which to live.

The fact that this is a *manual* prohibits a lengthy excursus on the narrative quality of Scripture, and, besides, there is a great deal of literature about biblical interpretation already. So I will simply note an example of taking cognizance of the narrative quality in doing biblical interpretation.

When Walter Wink uses his "new paradigm for biblical study" on Mark 2:1-12, he comes up with something like this:[6]

Situation: The "scribe" in me will not admit the "paralytic" in me,	*symptom*
so I remain paralyzed in some respect;	*result*
Complication: Because my "scribe" wants too badly to think well of himself to admit the "paralytic" in me;	*root*
Resolution: However, Jesus forgives the "paralytic" in me so the "scribe" in me can now admit the "paralytic" and still think well of himself,	*gospel*
so the "paralytic" can get up and walk.	*new result*

Sermon as Story

Not only is story the chief medium for the revelation of God in history, but it is also the chief medium for the communication of the gospel of God in preaching.[7] Every preacher might well adopt the hymn "I Love to Tell the Story" as a theme song.

Note that the model of the sermon as story does not refer to the inclusion of illustrations and examples, although this may be done. Rather, the concept of the sermon as story refers to the *whole* sermon, its content, its structure, and its dynamics.

If the sermon is told with sufficient description that the listener can say, "That's me; that's my story," the listener's own life experience provides firsthand examples for the sermon. So the concern is not to find examples to illustrate the sermon. Rather, the concern is to develop a sermon which illustrates, that is, sheds light on, the life of first the preacher and then the listener. On the one hand, this light is the painful light of exposure and judgment; and, on the other hand, it is the healing light of the gospel. Therefore, the often frantic search for illustrations and examples is obviated, and the frequent anomaly of anecdotes remembered but sermons forgotten is avoided.

A sermon which moved from the "spirit of loneliness" to the "fellowship of the Holy Spirit" needed no anecdotal example of a lonely person. This sermon's naming and describing the "spirit of loneliness" illustrated the examples of the "spirit of loneliness" which the listeners brought with them. In other words, the preacher provided the map, and the listeners, including the preacher, provided the territory. In the post-sermon discussion, people shared their territory examples of the "spirit of loneliness" and their experiences of the "fellowship of the Holy Spirit."

At other times, anecdotal illustrations and examples may be needed to communicate the sermon. If so, they should be used. But the preacher should be sure that they really map the territory of his or her life and are not merely pulled from a file to fill space in a sermon.

Pragmatics of Story and Sermon

If story is so important for understanding Scripture and for preaching the gospel, we had better tell the story and tell it well. In our culture, the pragmatics of storytelling has been developed primarily in relation to children. However, these techniques are also applicable to preaching to adults.

In her book on storytelling, Jeanette Perkins Brown asserts that "rarely is a person found, child or adult, who will not listen to a story."[8] But the attention-holding power of the story is only a means to the end of affecting human lives. So Mrs. Brown gives an illustration of how a story (or, in our case, the sermon as story) can avoid both moralism and antinomianism (see "Some Hermeneutical Doctrines" in chapter 4) and yet effect change in behavior. The example is about the way some Indian parents guided the behavior of their children:

> Abrupt commands to "Do this" or "Stop that" are not given. . . . They give the reason for the desired behavior in the form of a story in which the suggested action is portrayed, with the good or evil consequences to the doer, or the shirker.[9]

The "good or evil consequences" are included in the (old) result and the new result of our Dynamic Factors and for the same purpose. A story, like a sermon, has power to hold attention if it describes a world of people and predicaments with which we can identify. And, also like a sermon, a story has power to affect perception and behavior if it presents a new vision which grasps our imaginations.

We will illustrate how such power can be accomplished both in telling stories, drawing on Mrs. Brown's ideas and cartoons about the parts of a story,[10] and in telling sermons, using a condensation of a sermon with its parts correlated to the parts of a story.

As you follow the cartoons[11] and read the descriptions of parts of a story in the left-hand columns of the next six pages, correlate the story parts with the parts of the sermon which is condensed in the right-hand columns. That is, notice the correlation between the Introduction to a story and the sermon's Introduction. Next notice the correlation between the Action segment of a story and the Situation segment of the sermon. Then follows a correlation between the Conflict-Suspense segment of a story and the Complication segment of the sermon. Similarly, there is correlation between the Climax and Conclusion segments of a story and the Resolution segment of the sermon.

The previous correlations between the parts of a story and a sermon suggest that the pragmatics of storytelling and the pragmatics of sermon telling are so similar as to be interchangeable. The definition of storytelling by a second grade child which we quoted earlier might well be our operational definition of a sermon: "'It has to begin, and then'—making a quick gesture through the air—'it has to go right along. And something has to happen, and then it has to stop.'"[17]

In preaching, the central thing that needs to "happen" is *metanoia* or "repentance." *Metanoia* means, literally, a change of perception with its behavioral fruit. So, next, we will examine the power of stories and sermons which have the experiential movement of stories to effect *metanoia* or to "repent" (as a transitive verb) us.

Story, Perception, and Behavior

A number of recent studies give testimony to the serious impress of stories on perception and behavior, and, by implication, they give evidence of the potential power of preaching.

(continued on page 108)

Condensation of a Sermon
Illustrating the Sermon as Story
(Text—Psalm 56)

INTRODUCTION:
The first of the Psalms I read speaks of trusting in God and not being afraid.
I'd like us to think today about our *fear*
—where it comes from
—how it relates to our trust
(and finally) how trust in God truly enables us to be not afraid.

Parts of a Story
Correlated with Parts of a Sermon

The story's Introduction arouses interest and curiosity at once. It should be "not longer than a sentence or two. . . . It must give a clue to what the story is about. It anticipates, without predicting, the end. It suggests the problem which the climax will resolve."[12]

In a sermon, the Introduction serves a similar purpose. Our preacher picked up on the Psalms which she read as her texts and introduced the sermon as shown at right.

It arouses interest and curiosity at once.

INTRODUCTION

After the Introduction comes Action. The story goes somewhere. This part of a story is equivalent to what we are calling the Situation in a sermon.

The sermon will also move when it includes the five aspects of story which *story* carries in the cartoon, namely, (*a*) Plot, (*b*) Quest, (c) Journey, (*d*) Problem, and (*e*) Character.

It GOES somewhere.

ACTION

SITUATION:
As human beings
    we are *afraid.*
We fear because
    we are fragile, uncertain crea-
    tures in a world fraught with
    pride.
And we find ourselves in this huge
    and terrible world,
Alone and in need of a hand to
    hold, of something or someone
    to trust. . . .
So we look for something to trust.

. . .

For every step we take
    is a step into darkness,
        uncertainty, the unknown.
We do not know what the course
    of our lives will be, what God, in
    the span of our threescore and
    ten years, will require of us.
And we want to know; we need to
    know.

(*a*) In the Plot, the story begins with a situation in which the outcome is uncertain. The Plot aspect of story was incorporated into the sermon through the description of us as "uncertain creatures."

(*b*) In the Quest aspect of story, the characters seek something by which to resolve the uncertain situation. This aspect of story came into the sermon as the preacher described the quest for something to trust.

(*c*) In the Journey aspect of story, people face hindrances as they begin their quests. The sermon used the image of life as a journey with hindrances to be faced.

(*d*) The Problem aspect of story relates a person with a problem. In the sermon, the problem was stated as not knowing what the course of our lives will entail.

... the fear that comes with the experience of loss with the knowledge of the certainty of loss is a paralyzing fear....

It makes us unable to love or to trust

   to give ourselves to love others

   to share with others.

COMPLICATION:

However true our love for each other,

   however genuine our trust,

   the one sure thing is that

   the sharer of our love, our trust,

will some day be torn from us by death....

We will lose the very thing which we trusted to banish fears.

(e) In the Character aspect of story, a person's "feelings are so affected that a change in attitude (and consequent acts) takes place."[13] This is what we have been calling a change in word-perception-behavior.

The sermon incorporated this aspect of story by describing the feeling and attitude of fear and their consequent acts which need to be changed.

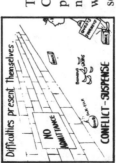

The Conflict-Suspense part of a story corresponds to the Complication in our nomenclature. In a story, "if progress is too easy, if there is no conflict, no struggle, if no choices are presented to make the outcome uncertain, we have only narrative instead of plot, not a story in the sense we are using the term."[14]

In the sermon, the Conflict-Suspense of the Complication has already been hinted at, but now it is made explicit.

But the preacher knew that the Complication was not rooted merely in the finitude of death. Rather, the complication was rooted in the "sin" of placing ultimate trust in something less than God.

The terrible fact is that
if we place our ultimate trust
in anything, in anyone
except God,
we are bound to fear.

So, in the sermon, the Conflict-Suspense is whether the person will place ultimate trust in something other than God and be bound to fear or place ultimate trust in God. The "evil consequence" of fear exerts the negative motivation for *not* placing ultimate trust in anything except God. The positive motivation of the "good consequence" for placing ultimate trust in God comes next, in the Climax.

The Climax in a story is what we are calling the Resolution in a sermon, especially the *gospel content* factor. According to Mrs. Brown:

"the most important step of all, around which the whole story creation moves, is the climax, the point of the story. Without a point there is no story. Each of the other steps leads to it. . . .

"If the climax is kept in one's mind, the effect will not be dissipated by the introduction of irrelevant details, or blurred by the storyteller's vague notion of what the story is all about."[15]

Matters reach a crisis.

CLIMAX

RESOLUTION:
He died because he loves us too
  much
  to abandon us to fear
  because he wants to show us his
  love
  so we can trust and not be
  afraid. . . .
So whatever we lose,
  we cannot lose everything,
  for we have his love.
We can trust in his love,
  and in his love we are not afraid.
God loves us so much that
  we trust that his will is for our
  good,
  that he makes all things
  —even our losses—
  work together for his good.
  We are in God's hands.

For we know his hand is there
  to hold us, to guide us.
We know that even when we lose
  much,
  we are in God's hands.

This knowledge of point and direction is just as important in a sermon as in a story. All the parts of the present sermon led up to the climactic affirmation of the one source of certainty.

The uncertainty of the Plot is resolved in the certainty of God's love.

The Quest is fulfilled, for we have found what we were seeking. The Journey's destination is sure with God to hold and to guide us. The Problem is resolved, for, even though we still do not know what losses we will suffer, we know in whose hands we are. The Character growth of changed feeling and attitude has been accomplished by the word-perception of the gospel. Trust in the love of

new
result
_____

So we rejoice.
We trust in him
and are truly not afraid.

- -

God has been engendered. The feeling of "fear" has been relieved. The attitude of being "unable to love or to trust" has been transformed.

The Conclusion of a story is a sentence or two giving a quick glimpse of what might happen next.

In a sermon, the conclusion might be designed simply as the end of the *new result* factor in the Resolution, or it might be added as a separate part. The present sermon added a two-sentence conclusion.

Way is now open for solutions of all problems

CONCLUSION

The sixth cartoon might be more aptly called "Peace" rather than "Listeners Relax," for, as Mrs. Brown describes this step, it is an active and creative rest in which the listener is "able to go back over the story at will, and find again its deeper meaning."[16]

And initial curiosity is satisfied. Minds are at rest.

LISTENERS RELAX

Children's Stories and Adult Behavior

In an article in *Science*,[18] S. A. Rudin reported on research by David McClelland and himself into the impact of stories on human behavior. McClelland studied children's books of stories from twenty-two nations for the year 1925 and rated them by countries as to the need for achievement they expressed. The impress which the stories made on the perception and behavior of a nation's population was measured by studying the economic achievement of each of the twenty-two nations from 1929 to 1950. There was a significant correlation between the need-for-achievement scores of a nation's children's stories and the nation's increase in per capita electricity output and some correlation with per capita income gain.

Rudin wondered whether this correlation between story content and technical behavior might not also hold in psychosomatic behavior; so he studied the causes of death in these nations for 1950. In the nations where the need-for-achievement scores were higher in their 1925 children's stories, the deaths in 1950 due to "inhibition" (ulcers and hypertension) were higher. In the nations where the need-for-power scores were higher in their 1925 children's stories, the deaths in 1950 due to "aggressive and acting-out" diseases (murder, suicide, cirrhosis of the liver) were higher.

Stories and Sub-Selves

George Brown describes an experiment in which a story was used to effect adult behavior. Behind the experiment was a conception of persons as composites of distinct sub-selves. These sub-selves either move forward into prominence or fade into background according to situations and roles. The sub-self in prominence "dominates the operation of the individual: his differentiating, his perceiving, and ultimately his behavior."[19]

The hypothesis was that "a symbol may be used to trigger a sub-self," in which case "the symbol would be a central core of meaning about which a sub-self has been built."

Subjects in the experiment were told a story about William Elephant who used familiar things in creative ways and Old Owl who always used things in conventional ways. When subjects were told to let the William Elephant part of them take the tests, they scored higher on creativity. The story served as a symbol to trigger the creative sub-self into prominence.

Stories and Growing Up

Psychiatrist Bruno Bettelheim has extolled the role of stories in helping children "master the psychological problems of growing up" by providing "answers" in imaginative perceptions which "scientifically correct answers" cannot. If the story is told with sensitivity for its "personal meaning," it can "communicate to the child an intuitive, subconscious understanding of his own nature and of what his future may hold. . . ."[20]

Similarly, telling the biblical story through preaching can help us perceive ourselves and our futures through the eyes of faith.

Stories and Consciousness

Professor Robert E. Ornstein distinguishes "two major modes of consciousness" (that is, knowledge or perception). One is the "verbal and rational" analytic mode of "science." The other is the "intuitive and holistic" mode of "religion."[21] Both are needed as complementary modes of knowledge; but the former has been dominant in our culture, so Ornstein pushes the latter. "Stories which function as word-pictures" are one means of communicating intuitive and holistic knowledge, stories which are not to be analytically "understood" but "to be absorbed into the very texture of your conscious being and your inner self."[22]

Then Ornstein asks, "How can these stories work on consciousness and communicate this way?" He answers:

> Teaching stories purposely contain certain specially chosen patterns of events. The repeated reading of the story allows these patterns to become strengthened in the mind of the person reading them. Since many of the events are improbable and unusual, the reading of the stories begins to create new constructs, or new "organs of perception," so to speak.[23]

In addition to the image of "organs of perception," Ornstein also speaks of stories serving "as templates for consciousness," an image similar to that of our verbal overlay map. Note the importance of a "pattern of events" here as we stressed the pattern of events in the biblical story as the structure for sermons.

These studies add evidence that "to tell the old, old story of Jesus and his love" can produce marvelous fruit in human perception and behavior.

Chapter 6

DYNAMICS OF
THE SERMON

We have already demonstrated the practical use of the Dynamic Factors. In this chapter we look at them more conceptually in relation to the dynamics of persuasion and human change.

In preaching there is a pastoral concern that all may be *changed* and "be transformed by the renewal of your mind" (Romans 12:2, RSV). In more functional terms, there is pastoral concern that the preacher and the congregation may be changed from some "sin" way of wording-perceiving and its "sin" symptomatic behavior with its consequences to a "faith" way of wording-perceiving and the resulting "faith" behavior and consequences.

Thus, this pastoral concern is first to help the congregation be aware of a "sin" word-perception-behavior complex and the resulting pain which might effect a desire to be changed, that is, the presentation of the Situation-Complication incorporating the *symptom, root,* and *result.* Then the gospel content is shared which might effect the change to a "faith" word-perception-behavior complex, that is, the proclamation of the Resolution incorporating the *gospel content* and the *new result.*

In this chapter we will examine the sermon in relation to us fallen sinners who need to be moved by preaching, who need to be changed. There are many biblical images for this change: for example, from being a bad tree bearing evil fruit to a sound tree bearing good fruit, from being an old creation to a new creation, from the mind of the flesh to the mind of the spirit (see Matthew 7:17; 2 Corinthians 5:17; Romans 8:6).

The five Dynamic Factors—symptom, root, result, gospel content, and new result—serve as clues for naming and describing factors in human change, factors which we believe to be biblically sound and which can be incorporated by the preacher into the sermon story.

The Dynamic Factors usually do not form the conspicuous structure of the sermon. Rather the Synopsis, with its two or three points in a story-like structure, provides the conspicuous structure. The Dynamic Factors are incorporated into the sermon story in an inconspicuous way. Nevertheless, the Dynamic Factors comprise the dynamic or power of the sermon. As Paul says of the gospel, "it is the power (*dunamis* or dynamic) of God for salvation . . ." (Romans 1:16, RSV).

A sermon can be verbally clear and, at the same time, be powerless because it does not incorporate these Dynamic Factors of change. So we will examine (*a*) the Dynamic Factors of change, (*b*) the person being changed, (*c*) a human change worksheet, and (*d*) various orders for experiencing the Dynamic Factors in sermon development.

The Dynamic Factors of Change

To get into the concept of the Dynamic Factors, begin by thinking of the person described in chapter 1. This person is a sinner who needs the transformation of which we have been speaking. This person is the preacher in the listening, hermeneutical, phase of sermon preparation. This person is everyone in the congregation when the sermon is being delivered. In all cases, the Dynamic Factors refer to human factors which a sermon might change. It is important to distinguish between constants and variables and between what can and cannot be changed through preaching in order to recognize the limits of what can be expected to happen as the result of a sermon.

Symptom

As persons we behave symptomatically in relation to ourselves and our perceptual world. In our fallen, "sin" condition there are always aspects of our behavior which are distorted and need gospel transformation.

Feeling-behavior is often the symptomatic factor which is most apparent as one enters first into the lessons and then into the sermon. However, one may get into the experiential story through the clue of another factor. In fact, feeling-behavior may not enter into a given sermon at all.

Action-behavior may also serve as a symptomatic factor for getting into the lessons and sermon. Often one will be able to identify with the actions of people in the lessons and say, "That's me."

Root

Behavior on the feeling or action levels is symptomatic of the underlying perceiving (or thinking or believing) level which is called, in our nomenclature, the root factor. Perceiving/thinking/believing is a function of the whole person, mind and heart. It is this aspect which needs to be changed by God's impress through the words of preaching.

The "from" and "to" of this change are set forth by Paul in Romans 8:6-8, when he contrasts setting the "mind on the flesh" *(phronēma tēs sarkos)*, which is death because the mind of the flesh is hostile toward God, and setting the "mind on the spirit" *(phronēma tou pneumatos)*, which is life and peace.

The word *phronēma*, translated "mind," means "what one has in mind, the thoughts and purposes." The verb form can mean "to direct one's mind to a thing, to seek or strive for," and it derives from the word *phrēn*, which means either "the midriff or diaphragm, the parts about the heart" or "the mind; the faculty of perceiving and judging."[1] Therefore, "mind" refers to that by which we actually live, not mere intellectual speculation. It might be called "gut" thinking or "heartfelt" believing which affects behavior.

The "mind of the flesh" is another idiom for the evil imagination of the thoughts of the human heart in Genesis 6:5. The "mind of the flesh" is another idiom for what we have called in this manual "sin" word-perception. It is our mind set in the state of original sin which was briefly described in "A Doctrine of Persons" in chapter 4. Bultmann describes not only the "mind of the flesh" as root but its symptomatic behavior as well when he writes:

> Whether, then, it is a matter of giving one's self up to worldly enticements and pleasures, either in frivolity or swept along by the storm of passion, or whether it is the zealous bustle of moral and religious activity that is involved—life in all of these cases is apostasy from God— a turning away from Him to the creation and to one's own strength, and is, therefore, enmity toward God (Rom. 8:6) and disobedience to the will of God (Rom. 8:7; 10:3; II Cor. 10:5).[2]

The "mind of the flesh" is the root which needs to be changed as the preacher works through the biblical interpretation. And it is this "mind of the flesh" in others which needs to be converted through preaching if we would have life and not death.

Until the particular root factor, the particular aspect of the "mind of the flesh," underlying the particular symptomatic "sin" behavior under focus is identified and described, it is impossible to hear or speak the gospel content effectively. This is true because our "sin" behavior grows out of the root. Trying to change voluntary behavior without changing the root of the behavior is futile, for, as Paul says, the mind of the flesh *cannot* submit to God's law (Romans 8:7). Trying to change behavior without changing the root is, in our Lord's analogy, as futile as exhorting a bad tree to bear good fruit. A bad tree cannot bear good fruit (Matthew 7:17f.). Even so, the root of behavior must be changed.

Furthermore, if the sermon proceeds on the symptomatic behavior level without identifying and describing the root of the behavior, there is no factor in the sermon which calls out for the gospel. Symptomatic behavior, in itself, only calls out for the law. There is also no factor which is open to receive the gospel. This lack of calling out and openness for the gospel in the sermon will be reflected in a similar lack of calling out and openness for the gospel in the listeners.

Sermons which end with moralistic exhortations or pietistic yearnings rather than the gospel are deficient. The preacher has remained on the superficial level of symptomatic behavior rather than digging into his or her life experience to identify and describe the root of behavior.

Result

Symptomatic feeling and action behavior result in consequences (or symptomatic feeling-behavior results in action-behavior and consequences). When the behavior is "sin" behavior, the consequences will be hurtful and deathly. If the painful consequences of our "sin" behavior are so described that we want to change (see Romans 7:24) and if the root of our "sin" behavior has been described and experienced, we are hungry to hear the gospel content as the answer to our plea.

When the sermon story leads up to the gospel climax in this way, the gospel is not heard as something which one ought to try to believe. Rather, the gospel is eagerly grasped as good news, for it frees the hearer from bondage to the root and its painful consequences. For example, in the first sermon example in chapter 3, when one suffers the pain of "hateful conflicts" which are rooted in attempts to establish one's "personhood," the gospel which affirms personhood comes as good news to be received with thanksgiving.

Gospel Content

The gospel content speaks an alternative to the "sin" root way of perceiving/thinking/believing. It might be thought of as the "faith" root for the new result of the gospel. Pushed by the pain of the old result and enabled by the gospel, we can cast off the old "sin" perception and put on the new "faith" perception. God the Word, speaking through the gospel content, can change our minds from being "minds of the flesh" to being "minds of the spirit."

It is important to distinguish between gospel and law. The law declares the imperative, which, if we obey, results in life. The justifying gospel enables faithful obedience. Law and gospel are both part of the biblical witness and of preaching. All of the example sermons in this manual communicate law. For instance, the sermon in chapter 2 communicated that we should give to the Lazaruses of the world and that we should not be afraid to do so by describing the painful results of acting contrarily. But the law and the gospel are not to be confused. The gospel is not spoken in the imperative—ought, should, must, etc. The gospel is not spoken in the subjunctive—if we try, if we believe, etc. The gospel is spoken in the indicative, and it makes "by God" affirmations. The gospel makes good news affirmations which are spoken "by God" and which are true "by God" no matter what we believe, think, or do. The gospel tells it the way it was and is and will be "by God." If the term "by God" can be used as slang to assert unquestioned belief in a statement one is making, surely the preacher can preach the gospel with no less conviction.

New Result

From faith rooted in the gospel issues the new result of transformed symptomatic behavior. Gospel perception effects gospel feeling-behavior, action-behavior, and consequences. One or more of these can be sketched out lightly in the sermon as the new result factor. However, the new result is left open-ended regarding details. An open ending makes the sermon more like C. H. Dodd's description of the New Testament parable: "arresting the hearer by its vividness or strangeness, and leaving the mind in sufficient doubt about its precise application to tease it into active thought."[3] In this way, the preacher avoids the presumptuousness of telling others precisely how to serve God. (Recall the Abraham Lincoln statement in chapter 2.) And, in this way, the dynamic begun through the Dynamic Factors in the sermon continues after the sermon has ended.

Note that the new result factor is not a "new moralism" or a "new idealism." Rather, the pressure of the painful consequences (God's wrath) and the new perception of the gospel (God's mercy) effect the new behavior. For example, in the sermon discussed in chapter 2, the new result of giving more freely to Lazaruses was not a "new moralism" that Christians who have been given so much by God ought to give in return. Neither was the new result a "new idealism" that Christians who have received from God will want to give altruistically to others. Rather, the new result issues from a dynamic both more radical and more realistic. On the wrath side, the threat of social unrest and the pain of a guilty conscience push one to give more freely. On the mercy side, the assurance of God's forgiveness and God's providence enables one to get past the twin fears of giving wrongly and of becoming a Lazarus.

The Person Being Changed

Having examined the Dynamic Factors of change, we now

examine more closely the person being changed. Our model of a person as a worder-perceiver-behaver can be described in five propositions.

We Perceive Through the Framework of Our Language

This formative role which language plays in our perceptions was reported by Benjamin Whorf in his linguistic studies. He observed that a culture's "linguistic system" was "the shaper of ideas, the program and guide for the individual's mental activity, for his analysis of impressions, for his synthesis of his mental stock in trade."[4]

Similarly, anthropologist Clyde Kluckhohn observed:

> Every language is . . . a special way of looking at the world and interpreting experience. . . . up to a point, one sees and hears what the grammatical system of one's language has made one sensitive to, has trained one to look for in experience.[5]

As preaching implants the language of faith, we will perceive through the eyes of faith.

We Behave According to Our Perceptions

Combs and Snygg find that "behavior is a function . . . of the individual's perception," and perception, in the comprehensive sense in which we are using the term, "includes all the universe of which we are aware."[6] Thus, our perceptions include things tangible and intangible, our physical and psychical experiences, our values and beliefs.

We Change Behavior by Changing Perceptions

As Combs and Snygg assert:

> To produce change in behavior . . . it will be necessary to produce some change in the individual's perceptual field. . . . Thus, the problem of changing behavior is not one of motivating people but of helping them to perceive differently.[7]

This means that preaching will most effectively change behavior, not by moralistic exhortation or idealistic appeals, but by proclaiming a new perception, a new vision.

Before continuing with the five propositions, let me insert an excursus about the complexity of word, perception, and behavior lest the model we propose seem too simplistic for life's complexity.

In the first place, the "Whorfian hypothesis" of the first proposition has serious critics. And, even for its adherents, "the Whorfian hypothesis is easier to accept intuitively than to prove in a rigorous way. . . ."[8]

In the second place, much of our behavior is directed by perceptions which we do not verbalize. In fact, "it would be placing an excessive burden upon language to expect it to convey fully the richness of images and perceptual experience."[9] The "preconscious foundations of human experience" have been investigated,[10] and H. Werner and B. Kaplan have developed a holistic model of "the symbolic process" which includes nonverbal "gesture language" and "linear expression" as well as "verbal code." It is "in terms of [such] different material media" that experience is "mediated."[11] Yet, nonverbal symbols have at least incipient verbal meanings. Whether perceptions are verbalized or not, language still plays a key role, and perceptions can be verbalized when appropriate.

In addition to perceptions which we do not verbalize, there are perceptions of which we are not even consciously aware, for example, when "playing the piano" or "driving an automobile."[12] But such perceptions can be called to awareness and verbalized. In fact, there is "increasing evidence that human adults do not learn unless awareness can be verbalized."[13]

The mystery of the dynamics of word-perception-behavior is acknowledged in a learned essay on the science of psycholinguistics. After delineating levels of linguistic function, the author concludes that "finally, at a level now almost invisible through the clouds, a listener may *believe* that an utterance is valid in terms of its relevance to his own conduct." However, understanding of the psycholinguistic processes of language and behavior is "still over the horizon."[14]

So it is that language functions with the mystery of Christ the ascended Word, invisible through the clouds, who yet makes his impress on us through the words of preaching.

In spite of scientific uncertainty, our model of human behavior seems at least not scientifically unsound, and it seems particularly congruent with the biblical Israelitic understanding of human behavior as summarized in Johannes Pedersen's *Israel*.[15]

In the Israelitic understanding, "when a man hears the word of

God, it is to be taken for granted that he acts accordingly."[16] The dynamics of this understanding are those of our word-perception-behavior complex. The word of God means God's expression of himself in and through historical conditions, and a "soul" (=person) is "stamped by the special conditions under which he lives."[17] The biblical term "soul" *(nephesh)* and our term "person" can be equated because, in biblical thought, "the soul [is] not part of man, but man as a totality with a peculiar stamp."[18] (A sermon might well be one of the historical conditions which stamp a person.)

As a person (=soul) has been "stamped," so he or she perceives and acts. A person makes use of "all senses," especially "vision and hearing," which "act together in one and constitute an immediate perception." This perception is by no means limited to the tangible for "one 'sees' heat, misery, hunger, life and death."[19] The congruence between the way a person words and perceives is recognized "when the Israelites . . . do not distinguish between *making* a man into something and *saying* that he is so."[20]

So the model of a total person with a total perception in a holistic, dynamic complex holds sway in biblical thought. "The soul is thus an entirety with a definite stamp, and this stamp is transmuted into a definite will." This is why in biblical thought and in our model it is to be taken for granted that when a person hears the word of God, she or he will act accordingly: "the will is the whole of the tendency of the soul" and "the soul can never exist without volition."[21] Said another way, Israelitic "thinking is to grasp a totality"; it is to grasp a total perception of the tangible and intangible. And "the essence of thought is . . . directed towards the action."[22] Action expresses the entire soul at the time. As a person has been stamped, so the person will perceive and act.

Affinity between this model and New Testament thought has already been suggested, especially in the discussion of the "mind of the flesh" and the "mind of the spirit" earlier, in which "mind" is roughly synonymous with "soul."

We Desire Change Only When We Incur Pain

Returning now to the five propositions, the next question is *how can perceptions be changed?* How can a person be moved from a "sin" word-perception-behavior complex to a "faith" word-perception-behavior complex? In biblical idioms, how can a person be changed from being a bad tree to a sound tree, from the old creation to the new, from the mind of the flesh to the mind of the spirit?

As long as I engage in a particular pattern of wording and perceiving, I will engage in a corollary pattern of behavior. In fact, I can voluntarily (freely, in this sense) behave in no other way, given the particular pattern of word perception at the moment. It is not that I am coerced to behave in a particular way. Rather, given the circumstances and given my pattern of wording and perceiving at the moment, I *will* to behave in one certain way. Flip Wilson's "Geraldine" captured the irony of this "bondage of the will" when "she" said, "Even when I do something I don't want to do, I'm doing it because I want to." Or as Combs and Snygg state it in their more prosaic style:

> . . . everything we do seems reasonable and necessary at the time we are doing it [although it] . . . may, in retrospect, seem to have been silly or ineffective. But at the instant of behaving, each person's actions seem to him to be the best and most effective acts he can perform under the circumstances.[23]

The catalyst for a desire to change is suggested in the above quotation. When a person begins to perceive certain behavior as "silly or ineffective," a psychic kind of pain follows, and, as Clinebell says, "People do not change until they experience pain in their present adjustment."[24]

This pain which accompanies "sin" word-perception-behavior, as interpreted in faith, is God's loving wrath. God's wrath may be thought of as operating on a person in three modes as "three pressures," namely, (1) "the pressure of his place in creation as a whole" (physical mode), (2) "that of his place in the society of men" (social mode), and (3) "the third pressure . . . of the man's own internal constitution and nature. . . ; that internal *Wrath* is what St. Paul understands by *conscience"* (psychical mode).[25]

These three modes of wrath are summarized in Deuteronomy 28:25-28:

> verse 25 "The Lord will cause you to be defeated before your enemies. . . ." (social mode)
> verse 27 "The Lord will smite you with the boils of Egypt. . . ." (physical mode)

verse 28 "The Lord will smite you with madness and blindness
and confusion of mind. . . ." (psychical mode)

As St. Augustine taught, this wrath of God serves a twofold
purpose. One is for "a just punishment . . . a suffering inflicted as
punishment." The other is for salvation: "a salutary pain that would
make you seek a physician" and which, therefore, "transforms the
bad, who are admonished, into the good, who may be praised."[26]

It is this second purpose of wrath which concerns us here—the
wrath that serves as a catalyst for a desire to change, a catalyst for
repentance. An example of God's wrath working through the social
mode to effect repentance is found in 2 Corinthians 7:9-10. Paul
refers to a letter which he had written and which "pained" the
Corinthians and confesses,

> . . . I am glad now—not glad that you were pained but glad that your
> pain induced you to repent. For you were pained as God meant you to be
> pained. . . ; the pain God is allowed to guide ends in a saving repentance
> never to be regretted. . . . (Moffatt)

In a sermon, the pain of God's loving, transforming wrath,
which accompanies "sin" word-perception-behavior, can be described; and this description re-presents the pain. This pain,
experienced in the sermon event, serves as the catalyst for a desire to
change and as the catalyst for a desire for the gospel content which
might effect the change.

In terms of the first sermon example in chapter 3, the relation of
God's wrath to the behavior which was called "hateful conflict" was
largely assumed and was verbalized only by allusion. The "hateful
conflict" was described as "fighting with the intent to destroy,"
"arguments which totally reject the other person," and "hatred of the
other person as the enemy." The isolation of cliques was implied. It
would probably have been more effective to have described the pain
of loneliness and fear and guilt which is inflicted on us when we
engage in "hateful conflict."

So, our *fourth proposition is:* We desire change in our wording-
perceiving-behaving when, and only when, we incur some form of
pain. Then we plead with Paul, "Wretched man that I am! Who will
deliver me from this body of death?" (Romans 7:24, RSV).

The deliverer, of course, is God in Christ Jesus who speaks and
makes his impress on us through the gospel content of the sermon. In

a sermon, it is Christ who effects the movement or change to the "faith" word-perception-behavior complex (or, in biblical idiom, to the "sound tree" or "new creation" or "mind of the spirit"). As Peter says, "You have been born anew, not of perishable seed but of imperishable, through the living and abiding word of God. . . . That word is the good news which was preached to you" (1 Peter 1:23, 25*b*, RSV).

The Gospel Gives a New Language of Perception

Thus, the *fifth proposition* is that we can be provided with new words which, when God the Father speaks his Word to us through God the Son with the power of God the Holy Spirit, reframe perceptions and thus designate new behavior. Again we refer to Combs and Snygg for experimental corroboration:

> . . . perceptions can be changed as a consequence of seeking new kinds of experience which will produce new kinds of perceiving. . . . Language provides a "shorthand" by which experience can be symbolized, manipulated, and understood with tremendous efficiency.[27]

In terms of the sermon example in chapter 3, the "faith" word-perception-behavior complex would be when, by hearing the *gospel content,* 1 word myself-in-the-world as, "My total personhood does not depend totally on any particular way of life but on my given identity as a child of God in which I am given my rightness as a person, the worth of what I do, and a continuing place-for-me."

Human Change Worksheet

The elements of sermon movement and human change which we have been discussing are often missing from sermons; so listeners say that "nothing happens." In order to clarify and test the movement of a sermon and its parallel in human change, the following Human Change Worksheet is presented. It is filled out for the first sermon example in chapter 3.

Note that the Dynamic Factors which engender human change are included in the worksheet as subtitles to the boxes. The essential change is from the "sin" word-perception to the "faith" word-perception, for, if that happens, all the other changes follow. Moralism tries to move a person with a "sin" word-perception to "faith" behavior by exhortation. Idealism tries it with altruistic appeals. Neither shortcut works.

HUMAN CHANGE WORKSHEET
showing movement in the sermon and in the person

"Sin" WORD/PERCEPTION (root)	CHANGE	"Faith" WORD-PERCEPTION (gospel content)
My personhood depends on maintaining my way of life; so a threat to my way of life is a total threat to my personhood.	Gospel content speaks to root and changes our wording-perceiving from "sin" to "faith."	*My total personhood does not depend on any particular way of life but on being a child of God in which I am given rightness as a person, worth of what I do, and a continuing place for me; so other ways of life are not a total threat.*

issues in → ↓ | | issues in → ↓

"Sin" feeling-BEHAVIOR (symptom)	CHANGE	"Faith" feeling-BEHAVIOR (new result)
Therefore, when I am confronted by another way of life, I feel totally threatened and on the defensive.	Change in word-perception effects change in feeling-behavior.	*Therefore, I feel less threatened and defensive and more secure and open.*

and ↓ | | and ↓

"Sin" action-BEHAVIOR (symptom or result)	CHANGE	"Faith" action-BEHAVIOR (new result)
Therefore, I will engage in hostile conflict to protect my way of life as if my total personhood were being threatened.	Change in word-perception effects change in action-behavior.	*Therefore, I can act more lovingly, criticizing and affirming values in differing ways of life, including my own.*

and ↓ | | and ↓

"Sin" painful-CONSEQUENCES (result)	CHANGE	"Faith" blessed-CONSEQUENCES (new result)
There follow destruction, rejection, enmity, and cliquishness.	Change in consequences follows change in behavior.	*(There follow more life, love, and unity in the Spirit who proceeds from the Father, through the Son who is the Word who speaks to us through preaching.)*

Experiencing the Dynamic Factors

In chapter 3 we displayed two forms of the Dynamic Factors Worksheet which demonstrated two common orders of experiencing the factors. But the factors can be experienced in many other orders. Following are some of the various orders to prevent falling into a rut of one pattern.

(1) We feel ____

    because we think/believe ____,

    which leads to action ____
      and to consequences ____;

  however, God says ____,

    and thinking/believing this gospel
    results in feeling ____, action ____,
    and consequences ____

(symptom)
(root) — sin
(result)

(gospel content)
(new result) — faith

(2) We feel ____

    and we act ____,
    which leads to consequences

    because we think/believe ____;

  however, God says ____,

    and thinking/believing this gospel
    results in feeling ____, action ____,
    and consequences ____.

(symptom)
(result) — sin
(root)

(gospel content)
(new result) — faith

(3) Because we think/believe ____,

    we feel ____

    and we act ____,
    which leads to consequences ____;

  however, God says ____,

    and thinking/believing this gospel
    results in feeling ____, action ____,
    and consequences ____.

(root)
(symptom) — sin
(result)

(gospel content)
(new result) — faith

(4) We act ____,

    which leads to consequences ____,

    because we feel ____

    because we think/believe ____;

  however, God says ____,

    and thinking/believing this gospel
    results in feeling ____, action ____,
    and consequences ____.

(result)
(symptom) — sin
(root)

(gospel content)
(new result) — faith

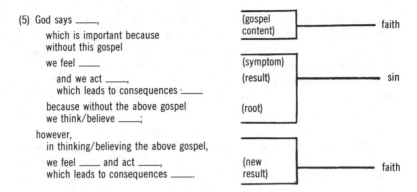

(5) God says _____,
      which is important because
      without this gospel
      we feel _____
          and we act _____,
          which leads to consequences :_____
      because without the above gospel
      we think/believe _____;
    however,
      in thinking/believing the above gospel,
      we feel _____ and act _____,
      which leads to consequences _____.

(gospel content) —————— faith

(symptom)
(result) ——————► sin
(root)

(new result) —————— faith

The Dynamic Factors might be experienced in still other orders, depending on how one experiences the lessons and how the sermon story begins to emerge. For example, the name "symptom" could be omitted and feeling-behavior, action-behavior, and consequences could be combined under the name "result." In a word, because the Dynamic Factors were conceived to facilitate the dynamics of the sermon as personal experience, conceive of them and use them in a dynamic and personal way—not mechanically.

A Concluding Word

The map of the Synopsis and Dynamic Factors given in chapters 5 and 6 contains many names and relationships. Yet, when correlated with the territory of human change, the map simply spells out common experiences: being influenced by a TV ad, the counseling process, the experience of a group as it finds new direction, talking with others about why we act a certain way and how we might change, the impact of an effective sermon.

For our map names we have drawn heavily on Scripture and on the language of the human sciences, especially in discussing the word-perception complex which underlies symptomatic behavior. I have used the hyphenated term "word-perception" because it seems most pregnant for a manual for preaching which is a "word" activity which seeks to influence the way we "perceive" as a means to affecting behavior. However, there are two alternative terms which might commend themselves as catchier synonyms for the clumsier "word-perception."

One alternative term is Kenneth Boulding's term, "image."[28] By "image" Boulding means one's total grasp of "knowledge," not only of "fact" but of "value" as well. His "first proposition . . . is that behavior depends on the image."[29] Therefore, to change behavior, the image must be changed. So, in communication "the meaning of a message is the change which it produces in the image."[30] Thus, we could say that the purpose of the preaching message is to influence the "image" by which a person lives and so affect behavior.

From the philosophical context, R. M. Hare coined the term *"blik."*[31] One's theory or frame of mind or what he thinks about the world is one's *"blik"* about the world. People behave on the basis of their *bliks.* Thus, we could say that preaching seeks to influence the *bliks* which direct human behavior.

So we can say "word-perception" or "image" or *"blik,"* but no matter by what terms they are expressed, the concepts contained in the Synopsis and the Dynamic Factors can save much time and futile effort. The concept of the Synopsis gives a direction to Bible study and sermon development. The concept of the Dynamic Factors gives clues to finding the power to effect change. I do not recall ever hearing a sermon with a clear Synopsis incorporating the Dynamic Factors which did not touch hearers with power.

Chapter 7

LITURGICAL CONTEXT
OF PREACHING

*This chapter views preaching in the context of liturgy:
the liturgy of Christ, the liturgy of the gathered church,
and the liturgy of the scattered church. Preaching will be
seen as an essential component in all three aspects of
liturgy.*

The English noun "liturgy" and the adjective "liturgical" are
often confined to denoting a particular type of worship. However, the
New Testament Greek ancestor word maps a much broader territory.
In this chapter we are using the broader meanings.

The Greek verb form of liturgy *(leitourgeō)* meant "to serve the
state at one's own cost; to assume an office which must be
administered at one's own expense; . . . to render public service to the
state." The noun form *(leitourgia)* meant "a public office which a
citizen undertakes to administer at his own expense. . . ."[1]

To render a liturgy, then, is to give service which benefits people.
As such, the New Testament applies the word to the work of both
Christ and his church.

The liturgy of Christ is witnessed to in Hebrews which speaks of
Christ as "a minister *(leitourgos)* in the sanctuary and the true tent
which is set up . . . by the Lord" (8:2, RSV). Comparing Christ with

the Mosaic priesthood, the epistle asserts that "Christ has obtained a ministry *(leitourgias)* which is as much more excellent than the old as the covenant he mediates is better . . ." (8:6, RSV). So the liturgy of Christ denotes his saving work.

In applying "liturgy" to the church, we will distinguish between the church as the "gathered" people of God and the church as God's people "scattered" in the world.[2] The gathered church denotes gatherings of Christian people in which they openly avow their identity as church. So, even though all members of a civic recreation board might be Christians, if they refer to themselves as the civic recreation board rather than as the church, they are functioning as the scattered rather than as the gathered church.

The Acts refers to the gathered church as "worshiping *(leitourgountōn)* the Lord" (13:2, RSV). And Paul speaks of himself as "a minister *(leitourgon)* of Christ Jesus to the Gentiles in the priestly service of the gospel of God" (Romans 15:16, RSV). Thus, the worship and preaching of the gathered church are liturgy.

The New Testament also speaks of the service of people scattered in the world as liturgy, without even being explicit whether they are Christians. Paul's justification for paying taxes is that "the authorities are ministers *(leitourgoi)* of God" (Romans 13:6, RSV).

The collection of money from Gentile Christians for the Jerusalem Christians falls on the boundary between gathered and scattered service. However the service is classified, Paul tells Gentile Christians that they ought "to be of service *(leitourgēsai)* to them in material blessings" (Romans 15:27, RSV), and that they will be enriched "for the rendering of this service *(leitourgias)*" (2 Corinthians 9:12, RSV).

So, service to God in the world, even when it is not owned by the doer as such, is liturgy.

Now we will relate preaching to these three aspects of liturgy— the work of Christ and of the gathered and of the scattered church.

Liturgy of Christ

The "once for all" saving liturgy of Christ is the gospel of God, its content, and its purpose. The content will be expounded in chapter 8, but for now the point is that the central purpose of the liturgy of worship, with its liturgy of preaching, is to make known the liturgy of

Christ. In fact, preaching is the primary and indispensible medium for making the liturgy of Christ effectively present.[3]

But how does a person dare speak of such a marvelous event? For that matter, how does a person dare speak at all? It is an audacious act to break silence. Silence existed prior to creation, prior to humanity, prior to speech. Silence recalls the beginning. It anticipates death. It fills every place from which it is not driven with its awesome stillness. Yet one person can utter one word and break it.

The audacity of breaking silence in the name of God to speak of God's liturgy for us is even greater. When the Lord was "like an enemy" at the destruction of his people, the elders kept silence (Lamentations 2:5, 10). When the Lord is like a friend at the redemption of his people, how dare we speak? How can we speak of "what no man ever saw or heard, what no man ever thought could happen" (1 Corinthians 2:9, TEV)?

We dare break silence because God has spoken to us from the silence. We dare break silence to speak the gospel of the liturgy of Christ because Christ commanded us to do so (Mark 16:15). We are taught that without the audacity of preaching people cannot hear and believe and be saved (Romans 10:13-14). We are reassured that we have the gospel treasure in ordinary containers like you and me "to show that the transcendent power belongs to God and not to us" (2 Corinthians 4:7, RSV). By the authority and power of God we dare speak the gospel of God. In the liturgy of the gathered church we celebrate and preach the liturgy of Christ.

Liturgy of the Gathered Church

Although the church gathers for ancillary purposes such as education, administration, and fellowship, the church gathers primarily for worship, and it is on worship we are focusing as the liturgy of the gathered church. We are approaching worship as a multilevel, multimedia communication complex in which God is the source and we are the responders. Through worship God impresses on us the faith story of his liturgy in Christ that we may believe. Therefore, I propose the following propositions about God, people, and worship as the context for preaching:

First, God is the initiator in the worship event. He speaks his Word to us, a Word which impresses and transforms. Therefore, worship as a human expression is a secondary response to God's primary impress on us.

Second, God speaks his Word to us through the media of actions and things as well as through the medium of words. Therefore, the widespread dichotomy between Word and Sacrament or between preaching and worship is semantic fiction. God speaks his Word through all media as an integrated communication complex.

Third, God makes his impress on us for the purpose of transforming us from the old creation in the likeness of the old Adam (that is, "sin" word-perception-behavior) to the new creation in the likeness of Christ (that is, "faith" word-perception-behavior). Therefore, we need worship. We need to be changed by worship. Worship is in no way an act of merit on our part or a device for changing God. Rather, worship is a gracious, pastoral, saving event which God in his mercy provides for us.

Fourth, God makes his impress on us through our rehearsing the marvelous things he has done, is doing, and will do through the liturgy of Christ as witnessed to in Scripture. If the biblical witness is communicated in worship as good news, thanksgiving (or eucharist) is engendered.

Fifth, as God makes his impress on us and our transformation is more fully effected, we worship less out of our need and more like the saints in heaven who worship in pure adoration.

Church as Multilevel, Multimedia People

Earlier we spoke of the biblical understanding of a person as "an entirety with a definite stamp . . . stamped by the special conditions under which he lives." Through these "special conditions" God communicates his stamp (= impress or Word) on various levels of perception through a variety of media, and his stamp is experienced on various levels of perception through a variety of media. To understand worship as the context for preaching, we will need further development of our "functional picture" of the person who worships. In addition to the word-perception-behavior complex, we will need to take into account levels of perception and the variety of media. This additional perspective can be schematized as follows:[4]

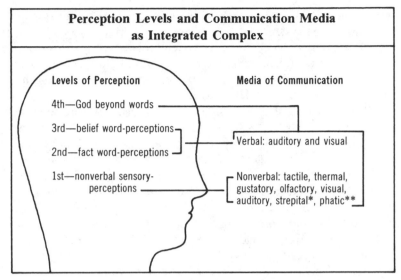

**Perception Levels and Communication Media
as Integrated Complex**

Levels of Perception	Media of Communication
4th—God beyond words	
3rd—belief word-perceptions	Verbal: auditory and visual
2nd—fact word-perceptions	
1st—nonverbal sensory-perceptions	Nonverbal: tactile, thermal, gustatory, olfactory, visual, auditory, strepital*, phatic**

*"Communicative body noise," such as hand clapping, foot stomping, whistling, yawning, etc.

**Vocalizations which are close to language in that they communicate general states of awareness and emotion but which, unlike language, cannot convey specific information.

Let me illustrate the schema with the story of Dick.

On the first level of nonverbal sensory perception, through nonverbal sensory media, Dick observed his research labs and production plants, his 5,000 employees, his $300,000 home, and the government officials with whom he negotiated contracts. Of such things Dick had direct and sensory knowledge.

On the second fact-word level of perception, Dick said things *about* the first level. He told his fact story: "I took the risks and I won. I borrowed money to go to college, and I made it. I took a job in a new industry, and it paid off. I quit my job and borrowed money to start my own plant, and I've succeeded. I know my business; I work hard; and I'm not afraid to take risks."

Dick was willing to amend his fact story. He would admit to being helped along by "a few good friends" and by "several lucky breaks." But on the third belief level, Dick spoke with adamant conviction. He was certain that the first two levels happened because "we live in a good system. I believe in our system. I trust our system. Do right by the system and the system will do right by you."

Dick's religious belief in the "system" made sense of his world and gave him confidence that his world would hold together. Dick was open and flexible about most things, but he would defend his belief in the system with desperation.

There may have been intimations of fourth level perceptions which contradicted Dick's belief story. He may have sensed that he was placing inordinate confidence in a human system. Could anything on earth be so trustworthy? Maybe he used vehement confessions of faith in the system to cover doubts about it. Or he may have sensed an inner emptiness. Could allegiance to an economic system be an adequate center for his life? If his life was so fulfilling, why did he need to keep telling his success story? However, if fourth level intuitions were threatening Dick's word-perception-behavior complex, he never admitted it.

Then the impossible happened. An anonymous bureaucracy changed procurement policy, and Dick's company lost its contract. Yet Dick could not believe the system would fail him. On the second level of fact word, he could readily admit that his company was failing. But to renounce his third level belief story would be to destroy his world with him in it.

So Dick revised his second level fact story about himself. Maybe he had not kept up with new developments. Maybe he had not worked hard enough. In some way he had not done right. He had failed the system; the system could not fail him. Dick was so psychologically dependent on his third level faith in the system that it was easier to destroy himself by second level accusations than to change belief.

I wish I could say that Dick has received fourth level intuitions which silenced his third level belief word-perception and changed it from faith in the "system" to the biblical faith in the God above all systems. But this has not happened. He recovered his lost contracts and reaffirmed his first, second, and third level perceptions. If fourth level intuitions threaten his idolization of the economic system, he still manages to suppress them.

My hope for worship and preaching is that through these media a person like Dick might be given a third level belief word-perception which is open to fourth level intuitions of the God beyond words, the God who is who he is, who will be what he will be, and who will do what he will do (see Exodus 3:14). The territory of this God puts to silence all the third level belief maps except those of his revelation.

And my hope for worship and preaching is that through them a person might be given third level belief which enables him or her to tell second level fact stories with neither arrogance in prosperity nor despair in adversity.

And my hope for worship and preaching is that a person might be given third level belief which enables him or her to enjoy first level sensory perception without feeling undue guilt or ascribing inordinate value to the sensory level.

Worship as Multilevel and Multimedia

The worship experience of Isaiah (6:1-8) encompassed almost all levels of perception and mediums of communication. On the nonverbal sensory level there were the visual, for he saw; the strepital, for the seraphim flapped their wings; the tactile, for the building shook; the olfactory, for the temple was filled with smoke; the thermal, for there was a burning coal; and the gustatory, for the coal was laid upon his mouth. Phatic communication is not expressly included, although it may be that Isaiah vocalized some nonverbal sounds. But the communication media on the sensory level were not ends in themselves. The sensory level provided the feeling tones and drama to enhance the second and third levels.

Isaiah spoke second level fact words when he reported Uzziah's death and told about the condition of himself and his people. Third level belief words were spoken by the seraphim.

On the fourth level, beyond even the words of seraphim, was the Lord. When the human King Uzziah, about whom people had spoken with inordinate trust for two generations, died and the people were put to silence, Isaiah intuited the King above all kings. Lower level word-perceptions witness to this God but cannot comprehend him. The verbal perceptions hold primacy over the nonverbal, but above them all is the God beyond words.

Turning from the Old Testament to the New, the Fourth Gospel displays an acute interest in the relation between the nonverbal sensory level and the level of belief. John views the proper role of the sensory, visible signs, as helping bring people to belief in Jesus. The sensory voice from heaven was given to help people believe (12:30). Seeing the raising of Lazarus was a means of belief for some (11:45). Seeing the risen Jesus and being invited to touch his wounds engendered faith in Thomas. The word of blessing for those who have not seen and yet believe seems not to disparage those who come to belief through seeing. In fact, John says that the purpose of the book is to relate signs (nonverbal media) as a means to bring readers to belief (20:27-31). Eating a breakfast of bread and fish renewed the disciples' faith in the risen Lord (21:12-14).

Congruent with Scripture, sensory perception as an aid to faith was stressed by Thomas Cranmer whose Book of Common Prayer has so widely influenced worship. Cranmer said that worship, by which we are "fed of God" with "spiritual food," faces the problem that although bodily life and nourishment are easily known "by daily experience and by our common senses," yet spiritual life and nourishment are "obscure and hid unto us." Therefore, Cranmer asserts:

> for this consideration our Savior Christ hath not only set forth these things [that is, the gospel] most plainly in his holy word, that we may hear them with our ears, but he hath also ordained one visible sacrament of spiritual regeneration in water [that is, Baptism], and another visible sacrament of spiritual nourishment in bread and wine [that is, the Lord's Supper], to the intent, that as much as it is possible for man, we may see Christ with our eyes, smell him at our nose, taste him with our mouths, grope him with our hands, and perceive him with all our senses. For as the word of God preached putteth Christ into our ears, so likewise these elements of water, bread, and wine, joined to God's word, do after a sacramental manner put Christ into our eyes, mouths, hands, and all our senses.[5]

In both Scripture and in Cranmer's rationale for multimedia worship, the nonverbal media are proper to worship only as they serve the verbal. In saying this, we do not despise the sensory. Rather we value all communication and perception, including the sensory, as serving God's Word.

However, there is a persistent tendency to disconnect nonverbal media from the verbal and give them inordinate value. In the worship of the Corinthian church, there were those who ate and drank the bread and wine merely for the bread and wine. Paul firmly reminded them that the bread and wine were intended to serve as media for the proclamation of the Lord's death until he comes again. Treating the nonverbal media as ends in themselves was not appropriate for worship (1 Corinthians 11:21, 22, 26). A century later, Justin Martyr still felt called to explain that "not as ordinary bread or as ordinary drink do we partake of them. . . ."[6]

Similarly, in John's Gospel, Jesus accused some of the people who participated in the feeding miracle of seeking him only because of the loaves as physical food, not as signs. So he told them, "you have seen me and yet do not believe" (6:26, 36, RSV). It was not enough to eat and see. For faith, it was essential to know what was eaten and who was seen.

Sermon Content in Context of Worship

When we preach in the context of worship, we preach within a complex of multilevel perceptions and multimedia communications. With this concept we appreciate all levels and media, but we do not neglect the peculiar third level, auditory, verbal contribution of the sermon. This integrated communication approach can be actualized in both content and delivery of the sermon.

Regarding content, we have already stressed the correlation of the sermon's verbal map with all levels of territory. Delineating levels of experience can help clarify not only the preacher's experience but the sermon content as well. For example, second level facts about how others evaluate us and the social and economic consequences thereof can be a big thing on their own level, and a sermon cannot directly alter their reality. So the preacher who assures the congregation that human judgment is a very little thing (1 Corinthians 4:3) should be clear that he is making a third level affirmation of belief and not a second level statement of social or economic fact.

More directly relevant to our present concern is the relation of the sermon's content to the levels and media of worship. This relation was suggested in chapter 2. It will be developed here through four examples: the sacraments (or ordinances) of baptism and the Lord's Supper, the seating arrangement, and the ritualized greetings.

John Calvin defines a sacrament as two-way communication, with God taking the initiative. From God's side, "a sacrament is . . . an external sign, by which the Lord seals on our consciences his promises of good-will toward us, in order to sustain the weakness of our faith." Then, from our side, "we in our turn testify our piety towards him."[7]

But how does one know what the visible signs mean? How does one know the content of our Lord's "promises of goodwill"? It is "the word . . . which preached, makes us understand what the visible sign means."[8]

So, speaking of baptism, St. Augustine said, "Take away the word, and the water is neither more or less than water. The word is added to the element, and there results the Sacrament, as if itself also a kind of visible word. . . ."[9] In the confluence of preached words (as well as other words of worship) and the sensory experience of baptism, a total communication of the gospel can occur. The sermon can so proclaim the promises of Christ's death and resurrection that our perceptions become immersed in the gospel and raised in faith as in baptism we are buried and raised with Christ (Romans 6:4; Colossians 2:12). The sermon can assure us diverse people that we each have a place in Christ's body as signified in baptism (1 Corinthians 12:13). Through preaching we may become "so possessed of the mind of Christ as in thought, feeling, and action to resemble him and, as it were, reproduce the life he lived."[10] In this way, the baptismal metaphor of putting on Christ becomes apt (Galatians 3:27).

The same kind of confluence of verbal and sensory perception is called for in the Lord's Supper. As Martin Luther explained the benefit of the sacramental eating and drinking:

> The benefits of this sacrament are pointed out by the words, *given and shed for you for the remission of sins.* These words assure us that in the sacrament we receive forgiveness of sins, life, and salvation. . . . These words, along with eating and drinking, are the main thing in the sacrament.[11]

By preaching, the gospel of the new covenant, which the cup seals by the blood of Christ, and the benefits of Christ's death, which the eating and drinking proclaim, are told in a present and direct person-to-person way.

Leaving the sacraments for less solemn activities, we turn to the seating arrangement and the ritualized greeting which is sometimes called fellowship time or, more formally, The Peace.

The congregation's seating arrangement, with most people looking forward in the same direction, can be observed by first level perception and factually described on the second level. But the seating arrangement can also be spoken of as a sign of the third level, a sign which conveys something of the fourth level. For example, resolution to "hateful conflict," as described in the first sermon example in chapter 3, comes as we each recognize our common dependence on the one God for our personhood. The sermon might well have suggested this meaning of our facing the Lord's Table together, waiting to be fed by him. Thus an ordinary sensory perception can become a medium for the content of faith.

Likewise, the ritualized mutual greeting is subject to first level nonverbal perception and to second level factual description. Third level belief language about it tends to be limited to humanistic concerns: the importance of interpersonal relationships. The interchange as a "kiss" of *agapē*-love, not *eros*-love (1 Peter 5:14), is often neglected. Thus the admonition of the fourth-century Cyril of Jerusalem applies today: "Do not think that this kiss is the same as those given in public by ordinary friends." [12] To the contrary, from one perspective the greeting is a sign of our unity in the loving mercy of God to us. As Paul says, Christ "is our peace, who has made us . . . one" (Ephesians 2:14, RSV). From another perspective, the greeting is a sign of our unity in the obedient commitment of our lives to God. As Antoine de Saint Exupéry once wrote:

> Life has taught us that love does not consist in gazing at each other but in looking outward together in the same direction. There is no comradeship except through union in the same high effort. [13]

Thus a sermon might reinterpret a merely interpersonal greeting into a sign of our unity in duty to the Lord who deigns to accept our service, as affirmed in the second sermon in chapter 3.

These examples are merely illustrative and suggestive of ways that preaching can fill the nonverbal sensory experiences of worship with meaning communicative of the gospel of God. By so doing, the total multilevel, multimedia complex of worship can serve the saving purpose of God's stamping us with his impress.

Sermon Delivery

As the nonverbal sensory media of worship are subsidiary to the verbal and join in service to the impress of God's Word, so in preaching, our bodies serve the message we want to share. In nearly all ordinary situations our bodies do this without self-conscious control. Pitch, volume, and pace of voice, along with demeanor, posture, and body tone, usually serve the message well. This is true until a person becomes self-conscious, as so often happens in preaching. Then the message becomes subservient to other concerns.

Maybe a person steps into the pulpit determined to be a certain style preacher, or determined not to be a certain style. Either way, concern for style supercedes concern for the message. Or maybe a person is so determined to do well that concern for one's performance supercedes concern for the message.

If we *read* our sermons, we are more likely to give precedence to concerns other than sharing the message because we can read a sermon even while thinking about something else. When a preacher is not totally involved in the message, the sermon sounds "read" because the subtle variations of pitch, volume, and pace which are present in the telling communication are missing. In contrast, if we preach without reading, if we *tell* our sermons from our minds and hearts, then our whole being becomes engrossed in thinking, feeling, and telling the message. When we are fully involved in telling what we want to share, we are less vulnerable to diversionary concerns, and our voices and bodies will express our involvement.[14]

In order to tell a sermon clearly and coherently, we must be able to *see* what we want to say—see both the parts and the whole. If we can see what we want to say and what we see forms a coherent whole, then with enough practice, we can learn to tell the sermon clearly and coherently. Then, whether we use a manuscript, outline, or nothing at all in the pulpit, we will not be reading words; we will be relating thoughts and experiences which we are seeing in mental images.

As an example of seeing the sermon, recall the "Rich Man and Lazarus" sermon in chapter 2. In the first part, the situation, I saw myself (and members of the congregation) as the rich man, surrounded by thousands of Lazaruses, each one pleading need, each one looking to us for help. Then I saw us fearfully recoiling from their pleas and clutching our possessions.

In the second part, the complication, I looked inside myself (and members of the congregation) to see the two-pronged root of the fear which makes us recoil from the Lazaruses. On one prong of the root, I saw the possibility of giving wrongly and thereby causing harm or incurring criticism. Then I felt the fear of giving wrongly. On the other prong of the root, I saw us giving to Lazarus and, by so doing, becoming Lazaruses ourselves. Then I felt the fear of becoming a Lazarus.

In the third part, the resolution, I saw Jesus coming to me (and to members of the congregation) in our fear of giving wrongly, and saying, "Even if you give wrongly, I forgive you, and I will make a good use of your gift." Likewise I saw Jesus coming to me (and members of the congregation) in our fear of becoming a Lazarus and saying, "I will provide for you and not even death can separate you from my care." As a result of these affirmations, I could see myself (and members of the congregation) being delivered from the fear, facing the Lazaruses more realistically, and making decisions about giving more rationally.

The sermon can be seen not only in mental images but it also can be mimed, danced, drawn, or acted. Each part can be seen in itself, and the parts can be seen together as a coherent whole.

In preparing the verbal content of the sermon, each part needs to be expressed verbally in a sentence which states the "point" being made in that part of the sermon. The points together form the Synopsis of the whole sermon. A Synopsis, which can be visualized both as a whole and in its parts, is essential for the kind of telling delivery we are describing. A Synopsis is essential whether it is written early or later in the process of sermon preparation and whether a full manuscript is written or not.

In preparing to deliver the sermon, the preacher needs to practice telling it until he or she can tell it fluently, making the points of the Synopsis, sticking to them, illustrating them by example and description, summarizing them, and consistently using the clue words of the Synopsis as the thought-bearing words throughout the sermon.

With such careful preparation, the preacher can see and experience what is being said as the sermon is being delivered. When one sees and experiences what one is saying, the voice and body will communicate the experiential movement of the sermon. The communication will be multimedia and multilevel.

As the preacher sees, tells, and experiences the sermon, she or he will be leading the congregation through the experience, part by part, until the whole sermon is experienced. Together preacher and congregation will experience the Lazaruses, the fear, the promise of Jesus, and the reduction of fear which leads to new behavior. This is the kind of telling communication we do most of the time. So the trick in sermon delivery is not so much to do something different. Rather, it is to do what we usually do naturally in a "supernatural" situation. When we are pastorally concerned with the people to whom we are preaching as sisters and brothers in the Lord and when we are engrossed in sharing a message which really speaks to us along with them, our bodies will nearly always provide the media necessary to deliver the message, and the message will nearly always communicate something of God's impress.

Gathered Church's Role in Preaching

This section will merely suggest some ways the church can contribute to preaching at three points: during, before, and after the sermon.

During a sermon, the church listens and responds, nonverbally in most places nowadays. The task of listening to a sermon is more demanding than preparing a sermon. As a receiver, a listener has to process the message at a pace set by the sender. There is no pause button to push or page to reread. As an interpreter, the listener must do simultaneous hermeneutics from the sermon to his or her own life. As a rememberer, the listener must retain a synopsis of the sermon for future reflection. At the same time, the listener contributes to the sermon by bodily response. The signals which the church sends back to the preacher can energize the communication loop or kill it.

Aside from the congregation's informal input before the sermon is preached, formal channels of input can enrich its content. An input group can meet with the preacher for a spontaneous study of the Bible readings for the sermon. Or the preacher can share his or her germinal thinking about the lessons to set a direction for the group's input. Or the preacher might share a summary of a sermon in process (something between a Synopsis and a full sermon) to test its relevance with the group and to reflect on implications. Or the preacher might want to test a full sermon. In addition to contributing ideas for sermon content, the group empowers the preacher with confidence by by the act of sharing their interest in his or her preaching.

After the sermon is preached, what content people heard and with what effect can be tested in a response group. Such groups not only offer continuing education in homiletics for the preacher, but also they provide valuable forums for lay preaching and faith sharing. As people tell the sermon they heard in their own words, they are preaching their sermons based on the preacher's sermon as the preacher's sermon was based on the lessons.

There is great potential benefit for preacher and congregation by the church taking an increased role in preaching. Thought and effort are essential, but there can be wider involvement, and there are some useful guides available.[15]

Liturgy of the Scattered Church

The church which gathers for the liturgy of worship scatters into the world for its liturgy of service to God. "If a preacher is to act on the world he must, as a rule, do it through his Church."[16]

That the preacher does, in fact, so act on the world was suggested in chapter 2. The sociologist Lenski was called to testify that the scattered church exerts "a far greater influence" than does the church gathered as an institution. And historian Butterfield was called to testify that "those who preached the gospel for the sake of the gospel, leaving the further consequences of their action to providence, have always served the world better than they knew."

In this section I will share personal testimonies of church folk which give credence to these general observations. These testimonies are only samples of those I have collected in interview-conversations.[17] They seemed to fall under three gospel affirmations.

1. Faith that God cares about what people do in everyday secular work increases moral concern and vocational commitment. (Recall the second sermon in chapter 3 for such a gospel affirmation.)

George manages a large financial institution. He testifies:

I think my work is a form of ministry. My association with my parish has helped me make decisions at my level that I should make, rather than pass the buck to somebody else. There is a tendency not to make decisions; you want to let somebody else do it. Through my relation with the parish, I am aware of this and am able to do it sometimes now, realizing that you take some risk in this and you aren't always right and you're certainly going to have people criticizing and you may even lose your job. . . . About two years ago, I really heard for the first time something I've heard all my life but never really heard and that was that Jesus did, in fact, die for my sins. I never had understood how somebody dying two thousand years ago could have possibly done that. But now I can accept that—and it makes me want to live a good life; it makes me want to live a life of thanksgiving; it makes me want to do good rather than evil. I don't know any other way to say it, but there is a lot of motivation for me in that.

Gilda describes her work as an elementary school teacher as a ministry. She says:

I try to work at the grass roots. My question is how I can help an individual student. If you direct your thinking toward service, toward ministry, in every individual contact with every person, God can work through you. You see yourself as being a part of his whole creation.

2. Faith that God cares about us and the people whom our work affects enables conscientious and courageous behavior on the job. (Recall the first sermon in chapter 3 for such a gospel affirmation.) Joan tells how her faith affects her work:

I work as a researcher-correspondent, which is a fancy way of saying I answer letters. I think my faith and my feelings for the individual person make a big difference in the way I deal with people at work. When I answer a letter, I figure there is a person out there for whom I might open a door. God cares about how I relate to other people.

Bob works at a large, commercial, medical-research center. Of his work, he says:

I am a staff person at the center, therefore I have some very fragile relationships with the major departmental people. I don't have quite the kind of line authority it is nice to have.

The church helped me in achieving an integrated staff. Finally, I just decided I really didn't care whether I got fired or didn't get fired. I thought that we should achieve a goal. In a year's time we were able completely to turn around and now we have about 25 percent minority employment.

What the church has given me, both from the worship service itself and from the personal relationships that I have with a lot of people in the church, is a self-confidence in myself that is irrespective of the job.

3. Faith that God is good enough and powerful enough to warrant entrusting oneself into his care for the outcome of one's life strengthens confidence and perseverance. (Recall the sermon in chapter 2 for such a gospel affirmation.)

Tom spoke of the tenuous nature of jobs in his company:

The pressure was on, not only from doing the job; but also as business fluctuates up and down, you begin to worry. You've got your family to look after; are you going to get laid off? We had a layoff one time of about 120 people when business really got bad. I can't do my work well in an emotional upset all the time. But I've learned really to cope with it. I'm not worried. I have more confidence because I believe in my God, Jesus Christ. And it helps me affirm that belief by being here. The preaching, the people, the little bit I have been able to do—all this has filtered into my life and into my job. I feel that, if I do my job as well as I can do, God will look after me. That's really my feeling.

Jenny ministers through personal contacts and volunteer activities:

I have been a widow for four years, and I live alone and I maintain a home. . . . I have been talking with friends about lay ministry and that's exciting to me to think that we lay people are important. Our everyday life is as important as coming to church on Sunday. Just talking to everybody—the bus driver, the clerk at the store, or just calling somebody on the telephone. A lot of people want to talk, to get things off their chests, and I feel that I am sort of a sounding board. I've enjoyed that. I guess that's what the Lord put me here for. . . . At church I feel refreshed. I feel that Christ is really saving me and I'll leave church and try again. It's such a reassuring thing to know that you are not alone in the world, that the Lord is with you and he does love you. At church you get that—that repetition. It gives you strength. People can't understand why I don't mind living alone or taking the bus or going out at night to meetings alone. I just know that God is with me; and no matter what happens, it's going to be OK. That keeps me from being afraid.

Such gospel affirmations, preached and heard as genuine good news, evoke a response of "Thank God." That is, eucharist is engendered. But Christian eucharist is not merely a feeling within the confines of the liturgy of the gathered church. Rather, Christian eucharist issues in the active service which is the liturgy of the scattered church.

For the discouraged preacher who thinks that preaching the gospel of the liturgy of Christ doesn't accomplish anything, taking time to listen to testimonies to the effects of the liturgy of the gathered church on the world through the liturgy of the scattered church might well provide cause to take heart and rejoice.

Chapter 8

FRAMED
AND REFRAMED
BY THE WORD

After recalling the power of words to frame and, more especially, to reframe perceptions, this chapter scans the content of the gospel word and its power to reframe us fallen people born framed by sin.

"The worlds were framed *(katartizō)* by the word of God," says Hebrews 11:3 in the King James Version. *The Amplified Bible* expands this to read, "the worlds [during the successive ages] were framed—fashioned, put in order and equipped for their intended purpose—by the word of God."

"The worlds" *(aiōnas)* might well be paraphrased, "all aspects of life, including human perception and behavior." The rest of Hebrews, chapter 11, gives examples of various aspects of human life framed by the word of God. The causative relationship between God's framing and human behavior is made explicit in the blessing "may he frame *(katartizō)* you for the doing of his will" (Hebrews 13:21, my translation).

In American slang, we recognize the power of words in human life when we speak of a person's being "framed" by false testimony. The "five propositions" of chapter 6 spoke of the power of words to frame and reframe perceptions.

Reframed by the Word

In chapter 6 we concentrated on the power of words to *frame* perceptions. In this chapter we are concentrating on being *reframed*.

"If you want to get well, you have to learn to use a language which more adequately fits the territory. The very structure of the language you are using helps perpetuate, aggravate and create neurotic symptoms."[1] Following this approach to therapy, the therapist (or preacher) assists people in learning to use language maps which more adequately fit their territory, thus reframing their perceptions.

In their book *Personality and Psychotherapy,* Dollard and Miller stress the critical role of language in therapy. "The neurotic," they say, "is a person who is in need of a stock of sentences that will match the events going on within and without him." The task of the therapist (and, again, the preacher) is to help people fill in the gaps in their "sentences" with "new verbal units."[2] Revised maps reframe perceptions.

Using Abraham Maslow's terminology, we need to be reframed from "need-gratifying" behavior to "self-actualizing" behavior. In the former, one's behavior is directed by attempts to fill unfulfilled needs, such as needs for "self-esteem," for "confidence in the face of the world," and for "being useful." Therefore, for a person to be "self-actualizing," that is, to act in response to the total situation without being bound by his or her own needs, the person must have received "basic need gratification." This "basic need gratification" can be "suggested" through "reassurance" and "improved understanding" from a "trusted" person.[3] The similarities between Maslow's two modes of behavior and Paul's living "according to the flesh" and "according to the spirit" are obvious. In both cases some form of preaching good news effects a reframing from one mode to the other.

Thomas C. Oden argues that all effective therapy depends on the communication of an ontological love which "says" to the counselee, at least implicitly, you are "acceptable as a human being by the ground of being itself, and that the final reality that we confront in life is for us—Deus pro nobis." This "implicit ontological assumption of all effective psychotherapy is made explicit in the Christian proclamation."[4]

Framed by "Sin"

We need the therapeutic reframing which preaching provides because of an inherent distortion of our nature, traditionally called original sin. The book of Genesis depicts this condition in the story of Adam and Eve, the synopsis of which typifies the structure of a sermon.

God created "man" as male and female, Adam and Eve. In the Garden of Eden, Adam and Eve lived in covenant with God, a covenant which included the prohibition: "of the tree of the knowledge of good and evil you shall not eat, for in the day you eat of it you shall die" (Genesis 2:17, RSV). That is, Adam and Eve were to live as "man" created in God's image.

> Just as powerful earthly kings, to indicate their claim to dominion, erect an image of themselves in the provinces of their empire where they do not personally appear, so man is placed upon earth in God's image as God's sovereign emblem. He is really only God's representative, summoned to maintain and enforce God's claim to dominion over the earth.[5]

But the threat of chaos hovered near the order of God's dominion. The worlds were framed from chaos and, if God let them go, to chaos they would return. If God let man go, he would return to the chaos of dust. If God let the garden go, it would return to the chaos of arid sand. So it is, as von Rad says:

> Man has always suspected that behind all creation lies the abyss of formlessness; that all creation is always ready to sink into the abyss of the formless; that the chaos, therefore, signifies simply the threat to everything created. This suspicion has been a constant temptation for his faith.[6]

In the Edenic situation, Adam and Eve could have trusted God to maintain them and the whole creation over against the threat of chaos. In trust they would obey the prohibition against eating the fruit. In trust they would not need to claim such knowledge for themselves.

The complication in the story arose when the serpent, who subsisted on formless dust, beguiled man—Eve first, as the receptive dimension of man; then Adam, as the responsive dimension. Why could not humankind live independently of God as the serpent appeared to do? Why could not humankind "be like God knowing good and evil"? Then Adam and Eve could trust in themselves and their own devices rather than in God to maintain them against the threat of chaos.

To be like God is to know good and evil in the sense of knowing everything from A to Z, from one extreme to the other. Such a claim to omniscience also lays claim to omnipotence, because without omnipotence there can be no certain knowledge of the future. And a claim to omniscience also lays claim to omnipresence, because otherwise knowledge would be partial.

The Edenic covenant allowed Adam and Eve to *touch* the fruit of the tree of the knowledge of good and evil. That is, they could legitimately claim a tentative knowledge of good and evil and thus legitimately exercise a limited dominion over the rest of creation. But the claim to possess within themselves, that is, to have eaten, total knowledge of good and evil was an arrogant claim, illusory and incommensurate with their true status as human and not God. Nevertheless, Adam and Eve were beguiled, and they made the arrogant claim until they realized that, by their attempt to possess everything, they had forfeited what they had.

There is a hint of the gospel resolution in the fact that, in spite of their arrogant sin, God did not destroy them. Instead he granted them a stay of execution and made for them "garments of skins, and clothed them" (Genesis 3:21, RSV).

This, then, is the Genesis story of the universal "sin" root from which we as preachers and congregation need to be reframed.

The Adam and Eve story and other biblical depictions of our sin give us clues as we join Luther in "the determined search for the rock bottom of his sinfulness."[7] At the "rock bottom," the root of sin is a deficiency of belief in God's gospel for which we try to compensate by "sin" behavior as Luther did before his conversion.[8] As we face what von Rad called "the threat to everything created," with a deficiency of gospel belief to allay the threats, we will inevitably "sin" by surrendering to the threats or by trying to ward them off using "sin" strategies.

We will now scan the *threats* of guilt, anxiety, and boredom; the *"sin" behavior* of trying to counter the threats without the gospel by either passive surrender or aggressive action; and the *gospel* of faith, hope, and love which actually allays the threats. Guilt, anxiety, and boredom, in relation to others, ourselves, creation, and God, comprehend the threats we face. The "sin" attempts to counter the threats cover the range of "sin" behavior, while Paul's triad of faith, hope, and love embraces the whole gospel.[9] Thus, what follows is a panoramic scan of "sin" and the gospel for preaching. The scope is comprehensive, but the illustrative content is merely suggestive.

The shape of this panorama of "sin" and the gospel may be diagrammed as follows:

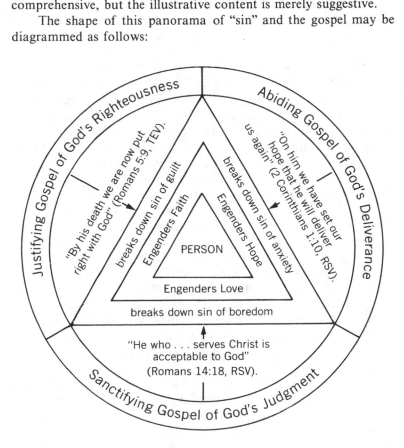

Reframed from Guilt to Faith

The feeling of guilt, whether called that or not, poses an almost universal threat. The feeling that something is wrong with me, that I am not good enough, pervades human awareness. Doubts about our OKness made Thomas Harris's *I'm OK—You're OK* a national best-seller.[10]

Undergirding the *feeling* of guilt lies the *condition* of guilt or condemnation. Guilt feelings are sometimes neurotic and unfounded, but more often feeling guilty rests on an actual condition of being guilty and deserving the verdict of condemnation for our "sin" behavior.

Two Orders of "Sin"

"Sin" behavior occurs on two orders. First order "sin" behavior inevitably occurs in our relation to others, in our relation to ourselves, and in our relation to creation—all in relation to God. Whatever life space we occupy for ourselves, whether it be a job or someone's attention, we inevitably dispossess others of that space. Yet we choose to occupy life spaces. In every choice, we inevitably deprive ourselves of other possibilities; yet we are the ones making the choices. Our very existence makes consumption of the creation inevitable; yet we choose to continue doing so. As Thomas Oden says, "Since human existence is a choosing existence, it is also a value-negating existence and therefore an existence bound up in guilt."[11]

Value-negating behavior is inevitable. Nevertheless, we are the ones who voluntarily make the choices. We are culpable; the guilt is ours and the condemnation is deserved. All of us are Adam and Eve: "There is no distinction, since all have sinned and fall short of the glory of God" (Romans 3:23, RSV). Thus, it is not only that "after one single fall came judgment with a verdict of condemnation," it is also that "one man's fall brought condemnation on everyone" (Romans 5:16, 18, JB).

First order "sin" behavior, since it is inevitable, cannot be prevented by the gospel. We cannot avoid the guilt of making value-negating choices. However, the gospel can reframe us from a much more serious and destructive second order "sin" behavior.

Second order "sin" behavior is more consciously devised to alleviate the threat of guilt (or, as we shall see later, the threats of anxiety or boredom). By second order "sin" behavior we try to gratify our need for "self-esteem" without the gospel. When we are "ignorant [or deficient] of the righteousness that comes from God," we arrogantly seek to establish our own (Romans 10:3, RSV).

Second order "sin" behavior, being not inevitable, is more calculating and devious and causes greater pain. The need to justify our actions, to counteract guilt, becomes the hidden agenda in all that we do and to that extent makes all we ostensibly do into a lie (Romans 1:25).

Relation to Others

For example, in relation to others, we play self-justifying "games," such as those described by Eric Berne.[12] Using a passive, hiding behind Eden's bush strategy, we play games like "Ain't It Awful" or "If It Weren't for Them." Using an aggressive, tower of Babel strategy, we play games like "I'm Only Trying to Help You" or "Look How Hard I've Tried." Of self-justifying strategies, Harris observes: "'Some of our best people' are where they are because of these efforts to gain approval. However, they are committed to a lifetime of mountain climbing, and when they reach the top of one mountain they are confronted by still another mountain."[13]

Our attempts at self-justification are finally self-defeating. Trying to justify oneself by rationalizations, explanations, or excuses not only alienates others, but also protestations of righteousness subvert one's credibility. Recall the judgment of Hamlet's mother when she saw herself being portrayed on stage declaring her never-ended love for her deceased husband: "The lady doth protest too much, methinks."[14]

When persons are certain of their own righteousness, their actions can be as destructive to others as the actions of persons seeking self-esteem. For instance, an issue of *Psychology Today,* commenting on Rollo May's *Power and Innocence,* editorialized on "The Savagery of Good Will": "Those who are *certain* of their *own virtue* but *innocent* about their impact upon others run the risk of becoming more irresponsible than the forces they fight."[15] The painful consequences of "the savagery of good will" consist not only of physical suffering but of mental torture as well.

On a larger scale, leaders of nations become so committed to the agenda of proving themselves right that they become blind to reality. For example, the initial involvement of the United States in Vietnam was in large part motivated by noble aspirations.[16] However, reality decreed that the aspirations, if achievable at all, would demand an exorbitant expenditure of money and destruction of life. But having publicly begun a course of action and invested in it, most of our national leaders were unable to admit being wrong. The threat of being condemned was too great. Instead, the "hubris" of self-righteousness maintained us on the original course until its painful consequences forced a change.[17]

Relation to Self

In relation to ourselves, attempts to reverse the threat of condemnation prove just as destructive. Edmund Bergler describes "psychic masochism" as a device for outwitting one's conscience by making pleasure out of punishment.[18] In his *Principles of Self-Damage,* he also relates the painful consequences which result. Many of the so-called accidents and errors we suffer are caused by a masochistic "guilt-plus."[19] Yet self-damage never removes the guilt.

Along a similar vein, Dr. Harold C. Morgan describes a more aggressive tower strategy. In "sin" attempts to make ourselves acceptable to others and to ourselves, we try to be *"super-*competent, *super-*intelligent, *super-*athletic, *super-*successful, *super-*sexual and *super-*Christian." However, we cannot be always super; so we are bound to suffer painful frustration. Then we may reverse the strategy and set out to prove that we are *unacceptable* by degenerate behavior. "But," as Dr. Morgan says, "man can no more prove his unworthiness than he can prove his worthiness."[20] Neither by behavioral perfection nor moral surrender can we prove ourselves "Not Guilty."

Relation to Creation

Examples of the deleterious effects of our self-justifying behavior on the creation have already been implied. We exploit earth and space to prove our worth in times of peace, and we ravage them to prove our rightness in times of war.

Relation to God

Using the levels of perception framework of chapter 7, we might say that our second and third level attempts to prove our righteousness by our performances for others and for ourselves can never fill the essential need to be "Not Guilty, by God." As Martin Luther failed, so must we fail to perceive ourselves justified before God by anything we can do.[21] Only a third level belief word, spoken with the fourth level authority of God, can provide a perception of acquittal by God from condemnation.

Gospel Affirmations

The gospel makes such affirmations of God's mercy to alleviate the threat of guilt. The gospel of God's mercy engenders "faith" in Paul's triad of faith, hope, and love: faith that we are justified by grace (Ephesians 2:8).

Scripture offers a rich spread of images for communicating the gospel of God's mercy.

> *the suffering servant:*
> He was wounded for our transgressions,
> > he was bruised for our iniquities.
> > > —Isaiah 53:5, RSV
>
> *a forgiving husband:*
> I will heal their faithlessness;
> > I will love them freely,
> > > for my anger has turned from them.
> > > > —Hosea 14:4, RSV

a loving mother:
"Jerusalem, Jerusalem, you that kill the prophets and stone those who are sent to you! How often have I longed to gather your children, as a hen gathers her chicks under her wings and you refused!" (Matthew 23:37, JB).

reconciliation:
In Christ God was reconciling the world to himself. . . . For our sake he made him to be sin who knew no sin, so that in him we might become the righteousness of God (2 Corinthians 5:19, 21, RSV).

verdict of acquittal:
. . . after one single fall came judgment with a verdict of condemnation, now after many falls comes grace with its verdict of acquittal (Romans 5:16, JB).

ransom:
He gave himself as a ransom for all men—an act of redemption
which stands at all times as a witness to what he is (1 Timothy
2:6, Phillips).

sacrifice for sins:
Christ . . . offered for all time a single sacrifice for sins. . . . by a
single offering he has perfected for all time those who are
consecrated (Hebrews 10:12, 14 RSV).

New Results

A gospel, which reframes us from perceiving ourselves as
condemned (1 John 3:19-20) to faith in God's mercy, transforms our
behavior and thus the consequences of our lives. We enjoy the new
results of being more able to attend to the people and tasks at hand as
we are freed from attending to the threat of guilt. So it is that the
gospel of justification effects sanctification of life.

Reframed from Anxiety to Hope

The threat of guilt attacks from the past. The threat of anxiety
attacks from the future. Anxiety is the awareness, often tacit, that all
we value is subject to destruction. It is the suspicion that, as Pascal
said, "The last act is tragic, how pleasantly soever the play may have
run through the others. At the end a little earth is flung on our head,
and all is over for ever." [22]

Sylvia Plath described anxiety when, pondering her future, she
wrote, "I saw the years of my life spaced along a road in the form of
telephone poles, threaded together by wires. I counted one, two, three
. . . nineteen telephone poles, and then the wires dangled into space.
. . ." [23]

Anxiety is tenderly depicted by E. B. White in *Charlotte's Web:*

"Summer is over and gone," repeated the crickets. "How many nights till
frost?" sang the crickets. . . .
The sheep heard the crickets, and they felt so uneasy they broke a
hole in the pasture fence. . . . A little maple tree in the swamp heard the
cricket song and turned bright red with anxiety. [24]

The feeling of anxiety is symptomatic of our actual condition
without the gospel. We are unable to prevent the destruction of
everything that we value. As our Lord said, "Heaven and earth will

pass away . . ." (Luke 21:33, RSV). And Paul echoes, "The last enemy to be destroyed is death. 'For God has put all things in subjection under his feet'" (1 Corinthians 15:26-27, RSV).

Two Orders of "Sin"

Anxiety may be thought of as inevitable first order "sin" behavior. In order to live, we must value others who will inevitably be destroyed; yet we make the choice. Our own lives inevitably suffer aging and death. Yet we choose to value them. In creation, as *Charlotte's Web* depicts, we value that which must inevitably be consumed by time; yet we make the choice. Our relation to God carries an inevitable anxiety that our beliefs may be lost in doubt or erased in error; yet we choose to believe. Therefore, as with the threat of guilt, the threat of anxiety is inevitable. Yet we call anxiety "sin" behavior because it results from a juncture of our choosing vulnerable values and a deficiency of gospel hope.

Second order and more destructive "sin" emerges from our attempts to alleviate anxiety's threat by our resources alone. As Kittel says in the article on *merimnan* (anxiety), we accept the illusion "that life itself can be secured by the means of life for which there is concern."[25] So we attempt to secure all that we value against destruction. When there is deficiency of belief in the gospel of hope, we devise "sin" strategies to supply our need "for confidence in the face of the world."

Relation to Others

Other people are sources of value for us, but they also threaten things of value to us. A strategy for evading the threat is to avoid commitments which involve others: nothing committed, nothing to be lost, no anxiety. So Allen Wheelis reports, "Commitments of all kinds—social, vocational, marital, moral—are made more tentatively. Long-term goals seem to become progressively less feasible."[26]

Another strategy against anxiety manufactures the illusory perception that our values are immortal. A diamond, and "a diamond is forever" says the ad, symbolizes interpersonal commitments. On his monument on the grounds of the United States Capitol, the late Senator Robert A. Taft is quoted (italics added), "If we can preserve liberty in all its essentials, there is *no limit to the future* of the American people."

Similar strategies operate between nations but on a level of enormous consequences. Reinhold Niebuhr described the passive strategy of pre-World War II Great Britain and the aggressive strategy of Germany. Both strategies were "sin" attempts to overcome anxiety,[27] and both strategies contributed to painful consequences of enormous proportions.

Relation to Self

Within ourselves, we use the two strategies to cope with the threat. A surrender strategy is illustrated in Ecclesiastes 4:2-3: "And I thought the dead who are already dead more fortunate than the living who are still alive; but better than both is he who has not yet been, and has not seen the evil deeds that are done under the sun" (RSV).

An active strategy is to meet the destruction of values with anger. For instance, a graduating senior addressed her commencement assembly:

> Traditionally, commencement exercises are the occasion for fatuous comments on the future of the graduates present. . . . My depressing comment on that rosy future, that infinite future, is that it is a hoax.[28]

An even more vehement retrospective anger was expressed in a letter to Ann Landers:

> Frankly, I'm surprised that more people don't kill themselves. For every ounce of pleasure in this lousy life, there is a pound of pain. For every good person there are a thousand scoundrels. Life is cruel and rotten and unjust.[29]

By referring to suicide, the writer points to a strategy which combines extreme aggression and extreme surrender in relation to oneself.

Relation to Creation

We consume huge amounts of the creation in irrational attempts to secure our futures against anxiety, attempts which range from military production and destruction to the use of unsound "health" products.

Relation to God

How the destruction of what we value can affect our relation with God is exemplified in a letter from a young woman, who wrote:

When I was a little girl, the world seemed so organized, so well made. I thought, "In all the beautiful order there must be a Divine control." And now I see chaos. I am very lonely and afraid. My mother is dead and my father hardly knows I exist. I am under a doctor's care. Where is my God of order, of justice? Is there none?

Is not God the destroyer as well as the creator of what we value? Was it not God who put all things in subjection under death? (See 1 Corinthians 15:27.) Does not God tell us,

> I kill and I make alive;
> I wound and I heal;
> and there is none that can deliver out of my hand.
> —Deuteronomy 32:39*b*, RSV

Again, he says,

> I form light and create darkness,
> I make weal and create woe,
> I am the LORD, who do all these things.
> Isaiah 45:7, RSV

Our God is the one who, as the potter, makes some of us vessels of wrath for destruction (Romans 9:21-23). No wonder that Job called God "cruel" and Jeremiah accused God of deceiving his people with false hopes and the writer of Psalm 88 accused God of casting him off.

Gospel Affirmations

Yet the gospel of hope affirms that it is this same God who will deliver us from the destruction which is anxiety's threat. How can we believe that he is good enough and powerful enough to deliver us?

We know God's goodness primarily through his being in Jesus Christ on the cross. We know the God who in Jesus Christ "has borne our griefs and carried our sorrows" (Isaiah 53:4, RSV). As P. T. Forsyth boldly states it:

> Christ . . . brings God's providence to the bar of God's own promise, His own Gospel. . . . He embodies the self-justification of God. . . . If any man thinks he has anything to suffer in the flesh, God more. In all their afflictions He was more afflicted.[30]

We know God's power primarily through his resurrecting Jesus

158 MANUAL ON PREACHING

Christ from the dead. As Paul testifies: "[Christ] . . . was crucified in weakness, but lives by the power of God. . . . we are weak in him, but . . . we shall live with him by the power of God" (2 Corinthians 13:4, RSV).

The gospel of hope, which counteracts anxiety, goes beyond the affirmation that God is really good and really powerful. The gospel of hope gives a new word-perception of ourselves and of our future.

First, we ourselves, our personhood, are ultimately grounded, not on values subject to destruction, but on the promises of God. Our Lord said not only that "heaven and earth will pass away" but also "my words will not pass away" (Luke 21:33, RSV). He not only exposes the foolishness of anxiety and our attempts to conquer it (Luke 12:13-21), but he also assures us of God's care (Luke 12:22-34).

We know that we have "no permanent home" on earth (Hebrews 13:14, NEB) and that we reside on earth as "aliens in a foreign land" (1 Peter 2:11, NEB). In the gospel of hope, we perceive that our "commonwealth is in heaven"; we are "citizens of heaven" now (Philippians 3:20, RSV and NEB).

Second, the gospel of hope promises a future. "I know the plans I have for you, says the LORD, plans for welfare and not for evil, to give you a future and a hope" (Jeremiah 29:11, RSV).

The future God has planned for us is so glorious that Paul says that the suffering of the present cannot be compared with the glory of the future (Romans 8:18). Scripture portrays this future as God's presence: "Now at last God has his dwelling among men! He will dwell among them and they shall be his people, and God himself will be with them. He will wipe every tear from their eyes; there shall be an end to death, and to mourning and crying and pain; for the old order has passed away!" (Revelation 21:3b-4, NEB).

New Results

To the extent our hearts are set on the heavenly treasure of the gospel of hope, a treasure invulnerable to destruction (Matthew 6:19f.), to that extent the threat of anxiety is reduced. As the threat of anxiety is reduced, other nations and other persons become less threatening to us. We respond to others more appropriately, more as self-actualizing persons responding to reality rather than to our own "sin" need-gratification for "confidence in the face of the world." We consume less of the created order in defending ourselves, and we destroy less of the creation in asserting ourselves against others. To the extent that the word-perception of the gospel of hope has grasped us, to that extent we can believe in the goodness and power of God and with thanksgiving accept the future he gives.

Reframed from Boredom to Love

"When I think how bored I am, I hate myself," screams a young adult.[31]

A review of a book on ex-pastors reported that "almost to a man the ex-pastors were bored with the endless round of trivia in the average parish."[32] *Newsweek* found "Boredom on the Job" important enough for its cover story.[33] Allen Wheelis listens to "modern man" and finds that "he is burdened by a sense of futility and longs for something or someone to give meaning to his life, to tell him who he is, to give him something to live for."[34] More recently, Bill Moyers observed, "I find a growing number of people who question whether anything matters, whether anything works, whether anyone listens, whether anyone cares."[35]

This is the kind of boredom we are speaking of—not the superficial boredom of a routine day or an uninteresting event but a radical and essential boredom—perceiving the very center of life as a "bore," that is, as an empty hole, a void. This kind of boredom is described by "The Speaker" in Ecclesiastes:

> Emptiness, emptiness . . . emptiness, all is empty.
> All things are wearisome [or boring?];
>   no man can speak them all.
> What has happened will happen again,
>   and what has been done will be done again,
> and there is nothing new under the sun (Ecclesiastes 1:2, 8, 9 NEB).

Two Orders of "Sin"

Boredom, like the "sins" of guilt and anxiety, is inevitable on the first order. The threat of boredom lies in the fact that there is nothing or no one on earth for which, in itself and for itself, it is worth spending the time of one's limited life. There is an innate futility about this world, even including people, because all are marked for death and destruction. Therefore, it is inevitable that in order to live on earth we must spend time on purposes which go down the bore, down the hole, down the drain. We inevitably spend some time of our lives on others who are slated to go down the bore; yet we choose to do so. We spend time on ourselves who must also go into the hole; yet we choose to do so. We voluntarily choose to invest our lives in a creation which is doomed to pass away. Even belief in God is threatened by boredom's emptiness; yet we choose to believe. So, although boredom is inevitable, it is "sin" behavior because it results from our choices coupled with a deficiency of the gospel of love as a vocation to God's service.

The "sin" root of boredom is this deficiency. In contrast to the gospel, the word-perception which underlies boredom sees spending our lives as "evil" in the sense used in the second sermon in chapter 3, namely, as "expressive of unremitted toil and carrying no suggestion of results." So it is true that "boredom is doubt," not an absence of things to do. If doubt about a sacred purpose in one's life were removed, boredom would be removed.[36]

But rather than removing the doubt by belief in a vocation under God, we often attempt to alleviate boredom by second-order "sin" behavior much more harmful than first-order boredom. Thus Søren Kierkegaard's "A" in *Either/Or* called boredom "the root of all evil" and interpreted history as attempts to escape boredom.[37]

Relation to Others and Self

Having recognized the evil impact of boredom, Kierkegaard's "A" devised a subtle method for countering boredom in relation to others and to self, using both passive and aggressive strategies. He accepted "change" as the cure for boredom, his own unique "rotation" method of change. His "rotation," as with crops, was not the "vulgar and inartistic method" of changing the "field." Rather, he changed "the crop and the mode of cultivation" by controlling his *"remembering* and *forgetting."* "A" was not a person who so "plunges into his experiences with the momentum of hope . . . that he cannot forget."[38] To the contrary:

> *Nil admirari* [to wonder at nothing] is . . . the real philosophy. No moment must be permitted a greater significance than that it cannot be forgotten when convenient; each moment ought, however, to have so much significance that it can be recollected at will.[39]

"A" avoided "sticking fast in some relationship in life"[40] like friendship or marriage because relationships which are valued are vulnerable to boredom's threat.

In spite of "A's" warning, attempts to counter boredom by the "vulgar and inartistic method"[41] of changing one's field are still prevalent. "The Speaker" in Ecclesiastes tried the pursuit of pleasure, and more modern "pleasure seekers" have carried on this strategy but, like "The Speaker," have found that "this too was emptiness" (2:1, NEB).

Even more "vulgar" boredom fighters have been dubbed the "thrill seekers." One observer of this strategy conjectures: "Action is the adolescent antidepressant. Thrill sports may just be a symptom of the depression of our times."[42]

More destructive than either the "pleasure" or "thrill" activities is the violence which, as Arthur Miller suggested in "The Bored and the Violent," often serves an anti-boredom purpose.[43]

Relation to Creation

In our attempts to alleviate boredom by our own devices, we also exploit the creation. We extravagantly consume earth's resources trying to fill the empty bore at the center of life. We devour an inordinate amount of the creation for products we do not need and which do not satisfy.

Relation to God

Our "sin" defenses against boredom's threat deny the presence of a God who cares what we do. What we call boredom, seventeenth-century theology called "anomie" or "disregard of divine law." Only by denying divine law and God's care about what we do can boredom be maintained.

An implicit denial that God cares was dramatized in the film *La Dolce Vita* (The Sweet Life). Frenetic attempts to fill boredom's void led to increasingly degenerate eroticism. At the end of the film, after the people had found that "this too was emptiness," they stood one morning on a beach looking across an inlet to another beach. There they saw a group of genuinely happy people—people who might well have known the presence of God. The erotic crowd looked wistfully across the inlet; as the film ended, they had not yet crossed the water into the new life.

An explicit denial that God cares about what we do was portrayed in the play *Waiting for Godot* in which Gogo and Didi surrendered to boredom. The opening line set the theme: "Nothing to be done." Actually, there was much to be done, for example, helping Gogo take off his boots which were hurting his feet. Rather, there was *nothing* to be done which was perceived as worth doing unless Godot came and imputed worth to *something* to be done. But Godot never came, and nothing ever got done. To remain essentially bored, one must deny the God who calls us to serve him in all we do.

All the "sin" strategies against boredom are condemned to failure. As Kittel says in the article on *mataios* (= futile, useless, to no purpose), the Septuagint taught that "there can be no possibility of being kept from nothingness unless it is given by [the] one God." The New Testament reaffirms this judgment:

> In the NT there is no mitigation of the ruthless comprehensiveness of the LXX. . . . Everything which resists the first commandment comes under the judgment of *mataios,* whether it be vaunting human thought . . . or the concrete gods of paganism, or the conduct controlled by them. . . .[44]

Or as Paul says in Romans 8:20, God has subjected the whole creation to *mataiotēs* ("futility" in RSV), until it is reframed by the gospel.

Gospel Affirmations

The gospel message which addresses the threat of boredom is, first, that we live under God's judgment. God is "lawgiver and judge" (James 4:12, RSV), and he cares about what we do. When we word-perceive ourselves as living under the judgment of God, what we do is stamped with an eternal significance. Our Lord says that "he who *does* the will of my Father who is in heaven" shall enter the kingdom of heaven. Upon his return "he will repay every man for what he has *done"* (Matthew 7:21; 16:27, RSV, italics added).

Similarly, Paul tells us that "God's righteous judgment . . . will render to every man according to his works" (Romans 2:5-6, RSV), for "we must all appear before the judgment seat of Christ, so that each one may receive good or evil, according to what he has done in the body" (2 Corinthians 5:10, RSV).

These affirmations of God's judgment are gospel in the sense that they announce the good news that God cares what we do. The assurance that God cares what we do, that there is *"something* to be done" for him, has the power to reframe us from boredom to works of love.

So Paul, in Galatians 6:9, after having said that we are judged, continues by saying that we are not bored in doing good, for in due time we shall reap satisfaction if we do not lose sight of the God who cares what we do.[45]

John Calvin boldly asserted that

> this life, estimated in itself, is restless, troubled, in numberless ways wretched, and plainly in no respect happy; that what are estimated its blessings are uncertain, fleeting, vain, and vitiated by a great admixture of evil.[46]

But, echoing Paul's image in 1 Corinthians 7:17, Calvin adds,

> Be ready at the Lord's will to continue it [that is, this life], keeping far from everything like murmuring and impatience. For it is as if the Lord has assigned us a post, which we must maintain till he recalls us.[47]
>
> Every man's mode of life, therefore, is a kind of station assigned him by the Lord, that he may not be always driven about at random. . . . He only who directs his life to this end will have it properly framed.[48]

Second, the gospel message, which addresses the threat of boredom, is that by God's mercy he accepts and uses what we do.

When, in Romans 12:1 (TEV), Paul exhorts us to "offer yourselves as a living sacrifice to God, dedicated to his service and pleasing to him," he does so because of God's great mercy to us. So, as Barth says, the exhortation in this passage "involves a perception of the pre-supposition of grace. . . ."[49] Barrett fills in this perception when he comments, "it is through these mercies, and not through any merit of their own, that men are able to bring a sacrifice to God."[50]

Thus it is that we can believe that God accepts and uses what we do even when our actions are not acceptable in themselves. We need to offer our lives to his service to fill the emptiness of boredom in us. We need a "by God" assurance of "being useful." The gospel of God gives us this assurance.

New Results

To the extent that this gospel is communicated with power, we are enabled to word ourselves as "What I do is accounted as significant and useful by the mercy of God." Thus we can perceive our actions as of value to God. When what we do is of value to God, life can never be essentially boring.

To the extent that we are enabled to word and perceive our lives like this, we will behave feeling not bored but invigorated and acting, not in hedonistic pursuits or compulsive labors, but walking in love (Ephesians 5:2).

Walking in love means acting lovingly in deed (1 John 3:18). Walking in love means acting in obedience to God (1 John 5:3). Walking in love means doing good works and serving others (Hebrews 10:24; Galatians 5:13). Walking in love results from having the emptiness of boredom filled with a faith perception of the vocation which God graciously gives to each of us (Galatians 5:6).

The Whole Gospel of God

We have scanned aspects of "sin" and the gospel one by one, but in practice all aspects of "sin" act in concert as a whole, as do all aspects of the gospel.

The Whole of "Sin"

Guilt, anxiety, and boredom complement and support each other in the totality of "sin" from which we need to be reframed by the gospel. "Sin" attempts to counter any one of the threats exacerbates another one.

The "sin" attempt to counter guilt by the fallacious word-perception that what we do does not matter because anything is permissible exacerbates boredom. The "sin" attempt to counter guilt by grasping for tokens of our OKness increases anxiety that the tokens might be destroyed.

If we try to counter boredom by idolizing what we do by saying that our actions matter ultimately in themselves, we increase guilt. If we attempt to fill boredom's emptiness with people or things, we increase anxiety over their loss.

If we devalue everything in order to allay anxiety over losing it, we intensify boredom. On the other hand, if we delude ourselves that what we do is of eternal consequence in itself, we intensify guilt.

Our mass culture's most pervasive "sin" remedy for guilt has been to foster the fallacy that anything we do is all right, by practicing a total "disregard of divine law" (anomie). Therefore, boredom has been diagnosed as our culture's most serious malady.[51] By trying to fill boredom's emptiness with things vulnerable to death we have exacerbated anxiety. So now we are trying to dull anxiety by thumbing our noses at death—Evel Knievel became a folk hero overnight. But death cannot long be denied; so we are being turned to a resurgence of moral concerns and to a renewed regard for divine law. However, unless moral imperatives are joined with the gospel of God's mercy, they will lead to other "sin" attempts to escape the threat of guilt.

The Whole Gospel

Faith, hope, and love also act in concert as a whole.

The gospel of God's merciful verdict of "Not Guilty" counters the threat of guilt and engenders faith. But this verdict alone does not counter anxiety, and boredom may well be increased if God's mercy is divorced from his holy judgments on what we do.

The gospel of God's goodness and power to deliver us from destruction protects us from anxiety over the end time by engendering hope. But hope alone does not speak to boredom or guilt in the "meantime" of our lives.

The gospel of God's moral concern alleviates the threat of essential boredom and so enables works of love for Christ's sake. But God's moral judgment alone heightens our guilt and may increase anxiety over whether we will be accepted into God's future.

From within the gospel, the threats of guilt, boredom, and anxiety are perceived as the left hand of God—his wrath—preparing us to receive the gospel which his right hand holds out. Thus guilt is perceived as provided by God to prepare us to hear the good news of our acquittal through the cross, which gospel engenders faith. Boredom is perceived as provided by God to prepare us to hear the good news that he mercifully accepts us and uses us in his service, which gospel elicits works of love. Anxiety is perceived as provided by God to prepare us to hear the good news that the victory is his and that by his mercy he delivers us from evil, which gospel engenders hope.

So the whole gospel is needed to reframe us from the "sin" of being turned in on ourselves, trying to protect ourselves from guilt, anxiety, and boredom, to being turned outward, responding in faith, hope, and love to the people and tasks which God lays before us.

Appendix A

SOME QUESTIONS TO ASK YOURSELF BEFORE PREACHING

Often in hindsight it is easy to see aspects of sermon development and design which were left undone and which should have been done. The following questions can serve as reminders to help you not leave undone things you ought to have done before you preach. You may not want to answer "yes" to all the questions. The essential thing is to be aware of what you are doing and why.

A. PRAYERFUL CONTEXT

1. Have I begun the sermon development process by offering my mind and heart to God in trust that he will speak to me through the Bible?
2. Have I carried out the process in an attitude of prayer in which I have listened through biblical human words for the Word of God for me?
3. Have I given thanks for the message which God has given and offered myself to him in trust that he will use me as one of his "earthen vessels" to communicate the gospel to others?

B. BIBLICAL AND THEOLOGICAL GROUNDING

1. Have I carefully read the Bible lesson(s), hoping to be grasped by a *movement* in it from some aspect of "sin" perception and

behavior to a converse aspect of "faith" perception and behavior and hoping to be struck by *clue words* in the lessons(s) which indicate this movement? (For example, from "strife, debate, and smiting" in Isaiah 58:4 to "love your enemies" in Matthew 5:44, in the first sermon in chapter 3, or from "days which are evil. . . , drunk with wine" to "walking circumspectly, discerning the will of the Lord" in Ephesians 5:15-20, in the second sermon. NOTE: In any given passage some part of this movement may be only implied or called for, so you may have to draw on the larger context of the passage.)

2. Have I tried to be relatively sure that I know what the *author* was saying in the passage in the *then* situation, especially through the clue words which indicate the movement which struck me in the passage? (Here is where you may need to refer to lexicons, commentaries, Bible dictionaries, etc.)

3. Have I listened through the Bible lesson(s), especially through the clue words which struck me, for a *message,* (*a*) which exposes an analogous aspect of "sin" *now* in my life-in-the-world, and (*b*) which renews (or reveals for the first time) some aspect of the gospel which actually effects some movement from "sin" perception and behavior to "faith" perception and behavior in my life? (This "listening through" takes time. You need to carry the message of the lessons around in your head several days and ponder it in your heart.)

4. Have I compared the message which I received through the lesson(s) to my *theological understanding* of God in relation to his world, including me? Does this message confirm or contradict any of my prior, functioning systematic, moral, or pastoral theology?

NOTE: Having received a message which moves you, you are ready to design a sermon which might serve as God's instrument to effect a similar movement in perception and behavior in the lives of persons who hear your sermon. The rest of the questions are intended to aid in sermon design.

C. CLARITY AND CONCRETENESS

1. Have I given a very *brief introduction* which gives the listener a hint of what I am going to say and establishes the clue words?

2. Have I made two or three *points* clearly stated in complete indicative sentences, which points together summarize the whole sermon in a synopsis?
3. Have I *illustrated* these points by description and example, on both the feeling and action levels, which speak to us in the here and now, so the points take on *concreteness?*
4. Have I used *clue words* from the lesson(s) as key words in my points, and have I stuck to these words and talked in terms of them throughout the sermon by using them to introduce and tell all illustrations?
5. Have I stated both sides of relational words and not left one side blank? For example, if I say, "We (or I) *believe...*," have I stated some content of the belief? Or, if I say, "We (or I) *doubt* ...," have I stated what affirmation is doubted? Or, if I say, "So and so has *meaning...*," have I stated the content of the meaning or the basis of meaning? Or, if I say, "The Gospel (or Jesus) *speaks* to us....," have I given some content of what is said?
6. Have I *summarized* my points already made before making *transition* to the next point?
7. Have I recapped the whole sermon in a *conclusion?*

D. IDENTIFICATION AND IMPACT

1. Does my first point describe and give an example of *symptomatic "sin" behavior* which makes an *identification contact* with me and which may also enable my listeners to make contact?
2. Does one of my points include a description of not only symptoms, but also the *root* of the symptoms, to give *insight* into the "sin" behavior under focus?
3. Does one of my points include a description of the *resulting consequences,* on both the feeling and action levels, of the "sin" behavior on which I am focusing?
4. Does the description of the resulting consequences move me to *desire to be changed* by the gospel from the "sin" perception and behavior to "faith" perception and behavior? Might it make a similar impact on those who hear the sermon so that they want to be changed?

E. GOSPEL CONTENT AND NEW RESULT

1. Does one of the points in my sermon explicitly and clearly speak *content* of the *gospel* which speaks significantly to me in *terms* of the *root* as I have described it?

2. Might this *good news* also speak significantly to my *listeners* in the facet of life I have described and in the same idiom that I used to describe the root? (The root should call out for the gospel and the gospel should speak to the root; for, as we have seen, the root of "sin" is a deficiency of the gospel.)

3. Has this good news *effected* (or reinforced) the *desired change* in my perception and behavior and might it do something similar for my listeners?

4. Have I done a *reprise* (an amended repetition) of the example(s) of the (old) *result,* the reprise being done in the light of the good news I am telling so the *new result* of the good news on understanding and behavior is illustrated?

F. CONTINUITY OF MOVEMENT

1. Do my points tell a *"story" which verbally and experientially follows* itself in a *continuity* without gaps?

2. Is the "story" told in my sermon *experientially true* to life? Can my hearers and I identify with and experience the *movement* of the "story"?

3. Does my sermon *move me* from a "sin" perception of a facet of life to a "faith" perception of the same facet of life so that new behavior might follow?

4. In its basic thrust, is my sermon in the *present* tense, the *first* person, and the *indicative* mood?

G. LUCIDITY AND DELIVERY

1. Is the overall *structure and movement* of the sermon, that is the Synopsis, so *lucid* that I can "see" what I am saying? Is it so lucid that I can dance, draw, or act it out?

2. Do I have the Synopsis of the sermon story in my *mind* so I know in my head (and not only on paper) what I want to say?

3. Does the Synopsis incorporate the *five Dynamic Factors,* namely symptom, root, result, gospel content, and new result?

4. Will the paper I take into the pulpit with me allow me to *feel*, *think*, and *tell* my sermon without being bound to the paper or to word-for-word memorization?
5. Will I be free from bondage to the paper so I can pick up the nonverbal *feedback* and clarify and restate the sermon as needed?
6. Is it likely that the hearer will get the Synopsis of my sermon *clearly* and *without confusion?*

Appendix B

SUGGESTIONS FOR
FURTHER READING

The possibilities for further reading in the areas on which the manual has touched are so vast that an extensive bibliography would require another book. What I will do is suggest only a very few books in each of six areas, often selecting readings which in themselves contain further suggestions.

A. PREACHING IN GENERAL

With one exception, rather than suggest books on preaching, I will suggest four sources for keeping up with books on preaching.

Recent Homiletical Thought: A Bibliography, 1935–1965, edited by William Toohey, C.S.C. and William D. Thompson (Nashville: Abingdon Press, 1967), is basic with 2,137 books, articles, and dissertations entered under 15 classifications. (A supplement from 1965–1975 is being prepared.)

Homiletic: A Review of Publications in Religious Communication (published semi-annually by The Homiletic Information Project, 3510 Woodley Road, NW, Washington, DC 20016) provides brief reviews of current books, articles, and dissertations.

The New Review of Books and Religion (combining *The New Book Review* and *The Review of Books in Religion* as of September, 1976) reviews many books pertinent to preaching. *Christianity Today* runs an annual Book Survey for the previous year in its first issue in March.

The book on preaching is Fred B. Craddock, *As One Without Authority: Essays on Inductive Preaching*, Third Edition (Nashville: Abingdon Press, 1979). It is a book on "method" which will variously complement, corroborate, and contradict this manual.

B. BIBLICAL INTERPRETATION

Hermeneutics, by Bernard L. Ramm and others (Grand Rapids: Baker Book House, 1971), is composed of ten brief chapters, each with a bibliography. (The contents of this book also appear in *Baker's Dictionary of Practical Theology*, Section 3, "Hermeneutics.")

For Old Testament interpretation, Foster R. McCurley, Jr., *Proclaiming the Promise: Christian Preaching from the Old Testament* (Philadelphia: Fortress Press, 1975) presents his principles and his method of interpreting the Old Testament for preaching and includes two sample sermons.

For New Testament interpretation, David M. Scholer, *A Basic Bibliographic Guide for New Testament Exegesis* (Grand Rapids: Wm. B. Eerdmans Publishing Company, 1973) provides a comprehensive, classified bibliography, annotated with evaluative descriptions. Dan Via, Jr., in *The Parables: Their Literary and Existential Dimension* (Philadelphia: Fortress Press, 1967) demonstrates doing New Testament interpretation through a blending of "historico-literary," "literary-existential," and "existential-theological" perspectives.

C. STORY

A good place to begin would be "A Symposium on Story and Narrative in Theology" in *Theology Today*, vol. 32, no. 2 (July, 1975); also James B. Wiggins, ed., *Religion As Story* (New York: Harper & Row Publishers, 1975). Both offer suggestions for further reading.

Speaking in Parables: A Study in Metaphor and Theology, by Sallie McFague TeSelle (Philadelphia: Fortress Press, 1975), collects many provocative ideas about story, Scripture, and theology. Her references make good clues to follow up.

The whole biblical story is simply and profoundly told by Theodore O. Wedel in *The Drama of the Bible* (Cincinnati: Forward Movement Publications, 1965).

Kenneth E. Bailey vividly amplifies and retells Lucan parables in his books *Poet and Peasant* (Grand Rapids: Wm. B. Eerdmans Publishing Company, 1976) and *Through Peasant Eyes* (Grand Rapids: Wm. B. Eerdmans Publishing Company, 1980) and in his talks on *Thesis* Theological Cassettes (P.O. Box 11724, Pittsburgh, PA 15228).

For many ideas about preaching as story, see *Preaching the Story* edited by Edmund A. Steimle, Morris J. Niedenthal, and Charles L. Rice (Philadelphia: Fortress Press, 1980).

D. DYNAMIC FACTORS

For a very readable introduction to the dynamics of language, perception, and behavior, S. I. Hayakawa, *Language in Thought and Action,* 3rd. ed. (New York: Harcourt Brace Jovanovich, Inc., 1972) offers what is becoming a classic. It includes an extensive bibliography.

Arthur W. Combs and Donald Snygg offer a more scientific presentation in *Individual Behavior: A Perceptual Approach to Behavior,* rev. ed. (New York: Harper & Row, Publishers, 1959).

Clement Welsh serves up the fruit of recent research palatably in *Preaching in a New Key: Studies in the Psychology of Thinking and Listening* (Philadelphia: United Church Press, 1974) and gives guidance for further study.

E. LITURGY

On the liturgy of worship, see Vilmos Vajta, *Luther on Worship* (Philadelphia: Muhlenberg Press, 1958), especially chapters on "The Proclamation of the Word" and "Faith and Worship." For a modern approach, "Liturgical Celebration, the Person and Psychological Health," in Robert W. Hovda, *Dry Bones: Living Worship Guides to Good Liturgy* (Washington, D.C.: The Liturgical Conference, Inc., 1973) is a good source.

On the congregation's role in preaching, William D. Thompson, *A Listener's Guide to Preaching* (Nashville: Abingdon Press, 1966) is very useful.

On preaching the sermon, William T. Kennedy, Jr., "Insights

from the Black Experience," *Thesis* Theological Cassettes, Volume 2, Number 5, is a good source.

F. GOSPEL CONTENT

For a biblical account of sin and faith, I find nothing to equal Rudolf Bultmann, *Theology of the New Testament,* Volume 1 (New York: Charles Scribner's Sons, 1955)—for sin, chapter 4, "Man Prior to the Revelation of Faith"; for faith, chapter 5, "Man Under Faith" and the section on "Jesus' Idea of God." For a more theological account of sin and faith with much illustrative material, see Thomas C. Oden, *The Structure of Awareness* (Nashville: Abingdon Press, 1969).

Many of the articles in *The New Bible Dictionary* (Grand Rapids: Wm.B. Eerdmans Publishing Company, 1962) proclaim the gospel as well as instruct.

Then there is the Bible itself—obvious, but too often neglected.

NOTES

References for Chapter Two

[1] This chapter is an adaptation of an article, "Preaching: What I Am About," which appeared in *Worship*, vol. 50, no. 3 (May, 1976).

[2] John Dyos, 1579, regarding preaching at St. Paul's Cross, London, as quoted in Millar Maclure, *The Paul's Cross Sermons, 1534–1642* (Toronto: University of Toronto Press, 1958), p. 146, condensed and spelling modernized.

[3] Stopford A. Brooke, ed., *Life and Letters of Frederick W. Robertson* (New York: Harper & Row, Publishers, 1865), p. 259.

[4] Bernard Berelson and Gary A. Steiner, *Human Behavior: An Inventory of Scientific Findings* (New York: Harcourt Brace Jovanovich, Inc., 1964), p. 550.

[5] Jeanette Perkins Brown, *The Storyteller in Religious Education* (Boston: The Pilgrim Press, 1951), p. 14. Copyright 1951 by The Pilgrim Press. Used by permission of the United Church Press.

[6] Marshall McLuhan, *Understanding Media* (New York: McGraw-Hill Book Company, 1965), chapters 3, 4, 5.

[7] David S. Schuller et al., *Readiness for Ministry: Volume 1—Criteria* (Vandalia, Ohio: The Association of Theological Schools in the United States and Canada, 1975), especially pp. 21, 22, 47.

[8] James D. Anderson, *To Come Alive!* (New York: Harper & Row, Publishers, 1973), p. 110.

[9] Karl Menninger, *Whatever Became of Sin?* (New York: Hawthorn Books, Inc., 1973), p. 228.

[10] Gerhard Lenski, *The Religious Factor: A Sociological Study of Religion's Impact on Politics, Economics, and Family Life*, rev. ed. (Garden City, N.Y.: Doubleday & Company, Inc., Anchor Books, 1963), section on "Religion's impact on secular institutions," p. 343. See also pp. 342-344.

[11] Quoted in "Fighter for Forgotten Men," *Life*, June 16, 1972. For Butterfield's

development of this idea, see his "Christianity and Politics" in *Orbis,* vol. 10, no. 4 (Winter, 1967), pp. 1233-1246.
    [12] Arthur W. Combs and Donald Snygg, *Individual Behavior: A Perceptual Approach to Behavior,* rev. ed. (New York: Harper & Row, Publishers, 1959), chapter 2.
    [13] Carolyn W. Sherif, Muzafer Sherif, and Roger E. Nebergall, *Attitude and Attitude Change* (Philadelphia: W. B. Saunders, Company 1965), pp. 228-230.
    [14] William J. Wolf, *The Religion of Abraham Lincoln* (New York: The Seabury Press, Inc., 1963), pp. 22-23.

References for Chapter Three

[1] In addition to personal observation, Edward T. Hall, *The Silent Language* (Garden City, N.Y.: Doubleday & Company, Inc., 1959), documents threats to personhood we are likely to feel when we try to relate to persons of different cultures.
    [2] Joseph Henry Thayer, *A Greek-English Lexicon of the New Testament* (New York: American Book Company, 1889), p. 116.
    [3] Cf. Michael Grant, *The World of Rome* (New York: The World Publishing Company, 1960), chap. 5, "Fate and the Stars."
    [4] Thayer, *op. cit.,* p. 530.
    [5] *Ibid.,* p. 279.
    [6] *Ibid.,* p. 318.
    [7] *Ibid.,* 220.
    [8] *Ibid.,* p. 24.
    [9] *Ibid.,* p. 285.
    [10] *Ibid.,* p. 605.
    [11] Recall that Sisyphus was eternally condemned to rolling a stone up a hill only to have it roll back down. Albert Camus hails Sisyphus as "the absurd hero" and claims that "the struggle itself toward the heights is enough to fill a man's heart" (Albert Camus, *The Myth of Sisyphus and Other Essays* [New York: Random House, Inc., Vintage Books, 1955], p. 91). If so, no gospel assurance is needed for the fulfillment of life.

References for Chapter Four

[1] Gustaf Wingren, *The Living Word: A Theological Study of Preaching and the Church* (Philadelphia: Muhlenberg Press, 1960), p. 209.
    [2] If this doctrine of persons seems too harsh, compare the description of "man" in scientific findings reported by Bernard Berelson and Gary A. Steiner, *Human Behavior* (New York: Harcourt Brace Jovanovich, Inc., 1964), p. 664: "He adjusts his social perception to fit not only the objective reality but also what suits his wishes and his needs; he tends to remember what fits his needs and expectations . . . he tends to hear and see not simply what is there but what he prefers to be told, and he will misinterpret rather than face up to an opposing set of facts or point of view. . . .
    "For the truth is, apparently, that no matter how successful man becomes in

dealing with his problems, he still finds it hard to live in the real world, undiluted: to see what one really is, to hear what others really think of one, to face the conflicts and threats really present, or, for that matter, the bare human feelings. Animals adjust to their environment more or less on its terms; man maneuvers his world to suit himself, within far broader limits."

[3] Bernard L. Ramm et al., *Hermeneutics* (Grand Rapids: Baker Book House, 1971), pp. 7-8. This paperback is a reprint of Section 3 of Baker's *Dictionary of Practical Theology,* ed. Ralph G. Turnbull (Grand Rapids, Mich.: Baker Book House, 1967), p. 99.

[4] Robert W. Funk, *Language, Hermeneutic and Word of God: The Problem of Language in the New Testament and Contemporary Theology* (New York: Harper & Row, Publishers, 1966), pp. 13-14. On pages 163-198, Funk interprets the parable of the marriage feast/great banquet (Matthew 22:2-10 and Luke 14:16-24), using a hermeneutical process very similar to the one this manual proposes, although he uses different nomenclature. His interpretation is recommended as another example of doing the hermeneutical process.

[5] See Genesis 6:5, RSV: "The LORD saw that the wickedness of man was great in the earth, and that every imagination of the thoughts of his heart was only evil continually." Such a heart is likened to "a root bearing poisonous and bitter fruit" (Deuteronomy 29:18, RSV; also Hebrews 12:15). This root of "sin" becomes imbedded in social orders as well as in individuals. Yet changes in social orders come about by the behavior of individuals.

[6] See C. A. Pierce, *Conscience in the New Testament,* Studies in Biblical Theology (Naperville, Ill.: Alec R. Allenson, Inc., 1955), pp. 69-71, and Deuteronomy 28:25, 27, 28.

[7] The organic connection between the *gospel content* (justification) and the *new result* (sanctification) is testified to by Karl Barth's essay on "Justification and Sanctification" in *Church Dogmatics, The Doctrine of Reconciliation,* vol. 4, part 2 (Edinburgh: T. & T. Clark, 1958): "The action of God in His reconciliation of the world with Himself in Jesus Christ is unitary. It consists of different 'moments' with a different bearing. It accomplishes both the justification and the sanctification of man. ... But it accomplishes the two together. The one is done wholly and immediately with the other." Although justification and sanctification "both take place simultaneously and together" yet "justification has to be understood as the first and basic and to that extent superior moment and aspect of the one event of salvation, and sanctification as the second and derivative and to that extent inferior" (pp. 501-502, 507).

[8] For descriptions of the "map" analogy in general semantics, see Alfred Korzybski, *Science and Sanity,* 3rd ed. (Lakeville, Conn.: Institute of General Semantics, 1948), pp. 750-751, and S. I. Hayakawa, *Language in Thought and Action,* 2nd ed. (New York: Harcourt Brace Jovanovich, 1964), section on "Maps and Territories," pp. 30-32.

[9] Our experiences usually feel so "real" to us that they seem to be unmediated absolutes. But the phenomenon which we call an experience derives from input as processed by the person. As Edward T. Hall says in his *The Silent Language* (New York: Doubleday & Company, Inc., Fawcett Premier Book, 1959), ". . . there is no such thing as 'experience' in the abstract. . . . *Experience is something man projects upon the outside world as he gains it in its culturally determined form"* (p. 111). Or as Korzybski says, "we read unconsciously into the world the structure of the language we use" (*op. cit.,* p. 60).

[10] This interaction of "map" and "territory" parallels the interpreter's "hermeneutical circle" and the "circular causality" of Gestalt psychology and phenomenology.

[11] Transparent = "Capable of transmitting light so that objects or images can be seen *as if there were no intervening material.*" *The American Heritage Dictionary of the English Language: Paperback Edition* (New York: Dell Publishing Co., Inc., 1970). Italics mine.

[12] The meaning *in* the content of the "map" and the meaning *through* the "map" as an overlay to the "territory" are characterized as the "mirror" ("with meaning locked *in* it") and the "window" ("with meaning coming *through* it") functions of poetry in Murray Krieger, *A Window to Criticism* (Princeton: University Press, 1964), pp. 3, 28-36, 66-69.

References for Chapter Five

[1] Gary Cronkhite, *Persuasion: Speech and Behavioral Change* (New York: The Bobbs-Merrill, Co., Inc., 1969), pp. 193, 197.

[2] Peter H. Lindsay and Donald A. Norman, *Human Information Processing* (New York: Academic Press, 1972), pp. 428-431.

[3] Stephen Crites, "The Narrative Quality of Experience," *Journal of the American Academy of Religion,* vol. 39 (1971), pp. 291-311.

[4] G. Ernest Wright, *God Who Acts: Biblical Theology as Recital,* Studies in Biblical Theology, (London: SCM Press, 1952), p. 13.

[5] Theodore O. Wedel, *The Drama of the Bible* (Cincinnati: Forward Movement Publications, 1965), p. 17.

[6] Walter Wink, *The Bible in Human Transformation: Toward a New Paradigm for Biblical Study* (Philadelphia: Fortress Press, 1973), pp. 54-58.

[7] H. Richard Niebuhr, *The Meaning of Revelation* (New York: Macmillan Inc., 1941), pp. 46-48; see also Robert P. Roth, *Story and Reality: An Essay on Truth* (Grand Rapids: Wm. B. Eerdmans Publishing Company, 1973), pp. 12 and 87.

[8] Jeanette Perkins Brown, *The Storyteller in Religious Education: How to Tell Stories to Children and Young People* (Boston: The Pilgrim Press, 1951), p. vi.

[9] *Ibid.,* p. 2.

[10] The cartoons are from Brown, *The Storyteller. . . ,* frontispiece. They first appeared in "Child Guidance," published by the Methodist Publishing House, Copyright 1946, then in "Children's Religion," published by The Pilgrim Press. They have been adapted by Hugh Williams for this book through the courtesy of the publishers.

[11] The sermon was preached by Sharon Lloyd Sullivan in Homiletics One at the Episcopal Theological Seminary in Virginia.

[12] Brown, *op. cit.,* p. 17.

[13] *Ibid.,* p. 16.

[14] *Ibid.,* pp. 21f.

[15] *Ibid.,* p. 14.

[16] *Ibid.,* p. 23.

[17] *Ibid.,* p. 14.

[18] S. A. Rudin, "National Motives Predict Psychogenic Death Rates 25 Years Later," *Science,* vol. 160 (May 24, 1968), pp. 901-903. See also David C. McClelland, *The Achieving Society* (Princeton: D. Van Nostrand Company, 1961).

[19] George Brown, "The Creative Sub-Self" in Herbert A. Otto and John Mann,

eds., *Ways of Growth* (New York: Grossman Publishers, 1968), pp. 147-157, especially pp. 151-152.

[20] Bruno Bettelheim, "The Uses of Enchantment," *The New Yorker,* December 8, 1975, pp. 50-114. For a fuller exposition of his ideas, see Bruno Bettelheim, *The Uses of Enchantment: The Meaning and Importance of Fairy Tales* (New York: Alfred A. Knopf, Inc., 1976).

[21] Robert E. Ornstein, *The Psychology of Consciousness* (New York: The Viking Press, 1972), pp. 10, 163, 170-178, 184.

[22] *Ibid.,* pp. 169-170 (a quote from Rafael Lefort, *The Teachers of Gurdjieff* [London: Gollancz, 1968], p. 57).

[23] *Ibid.,* p. 171.

References for Chapter Six

[1] Joseph Henry Thayer, *Greek-English Lexicon of the New Testament* (New York: American Book Company, 1889), p. 658.

[2] Rudolf Bultmann, *Theology of the New Testament* (New York: Charles Scribner's Sons, 1951), vol. 1, p. 241.

[3] C. H. Dodd, *The Parables of the Kingdom, 3rd. ed.* (London: Nisbet & Co., Ltd., 1936), p. 16.

[4] Benjamin Whorf, "Science and Linguistics," in *Language, Thought, and Reality: Selected Writings of Benjamin Lee Whorf,* edited by John B. Carroll (Cambridge: The M.I.T. Press, 1964), p. 212.

[5] Clyde Kluckhohn, *Mirror for Man* (New York: McGraw-Hill Book Company, 1949), p. 159.

[6] Arthur W. Combs and Donald Snygg, *Individual Behavior: A Perceptual Approach to Behavior* (New York: Harper & Row, Publishers, 1959), pp. 21-22.

[7] *Ibid.,* pp. 36, 57.

[8] *International Encyclopedia of the Social Sciences (I. E. S. S.)* (New York: Macmillan and the Free Press, 1968), vol. 9, p. 22a.

[9] *I.E.S.S.,* vol. 11, p. 576b.

[10] Trigant Burrow, *Preconscious Foundations of Human Experience* (New York: Basic Books, Inc., Publishers, 1964).

[11] Heinz Werner and Bernard Kaplan, "Symbolic Mediation and Organization of Thought: An Experimental Approach by Means of the Line-Schematization Technique," *Journal of Psychology,* vol. 43 (1957), pp. 3-25. See also Heinz Werner and Bernard Kaplan, *Symbol Formation: An Organismic-Developmental Approach to Language and the Expression of Thought* (New York: John Wiley & Sons, Inc., 1963).

[12] *I.E.S.S.,* vol. 11, p. 579b.

[13] *Ibid.,* p. 580b.

[14] George A. Miller, "The Psycholinguists: On the New Scientists of Language," in *Psycholinguistics: A Survey of Theory and Research Problems,* ed. Charles E. Osgood and Thomas A. Sebeok (Bloomington: Indiana University Press, 1965), p. 295.

[15] Johannes Pedersen, *Israel* (London: Geoffrey Cumberlege, Oxford University Press, 1926), vol. 1, section on "The Soul, Its Powers and Capacity," pp. 99-181.

[16] *Ibid.*, p. 132.
[17] *Ibid.*, p. 100.
[18] *Ibid.*, p. 11.
[19] *Ibid.*, p. 100. See "preceptual field," page 117 of this book.
[20] *Ibid.*, p. 167.
[21] *Ibid.*, p. 103.
[22] *Ibid.*, pp. 108, 128.
[23] Combs and Snygg, *op. cit.*, p. 17.
[24] Howard J. Clinebell, Jr., *Basic Types of Pastoral Counseling* (Nashville: Abingdon Press, 1966), p. 226.
[25] C. A. Pierce, *Conscience in the New Testament*, Studies in Biblical Theology (Naperville, Ill.: Alec R. Allenson, Inc., 1955), pp. 69-70.
[26] Saint Augustine, *Admonition and Grace*, 2nd. ed. (New York: Fathers of the Church, Inc., 1950), 5(7), p. 251, and 14(43), p. 297.
[27] Combs and Snygg, *op. cit.*, pp. 356, 134.
[28] Kenneth E. Boulding, *The Image* (Ann Arbor: University of Michigan Press, 1956), especially chapter 1.
[29] *Ibid.*, p. 6, in italics.
[30] *Ibid.*, p. 7, in italics.
[31] R. M. Hare, Section B of "Theology and Falsification," in Antony Flew and Alasdair MacIntyre, eds., *New Essays in Philosophical Theology* (London: SCM Press, 1955), pp. 99-103.

References for Chapter Seven

[1] Joseph Henry Thayer, *Greek-English Lexicon of the New Testament* (New York: American Book Company, 1889), p. 375.
[2] Hans-Ruedi Weber, *Salty Christians* (New York: The Seabury Press, Inc., 1963), pp. 9-18.
[3] Rudolf Bultmann, *Theology of the New Testament* (New York: Charles Scribner's Sons, 1951), vol. 1, pp. 302, 306.
[4] For the structure of levels of perception, I am indebted to the concept of "multiordinality" in Alfred Korzybski, *Science and Sanity*, 3rd ed. (Lakeville, Conn.: Institute of General Semantics, 1948), and to the "orders of knowledge" in Paul Watzlawick et al., *Pragmatics of Human Communication* (New York: W. W. Norton & Company, Inc., 1967), pp. 260-267. For the media of communication, I am indebted to Roger W. Wescott, "Introducing Coenetics: A Biosocial Analysis of Communication," *The American Scholar*, vol. 35 (1966), pp. 342-356.
[5] Thomas Cranmer, *An Answer Unto A Crafty And Sophistical Cavillation Devised By Stephen Gardiner. . .*, in the *Writings And Disputations Of Thomas Cranmer Relative To The Sacrament Of The Lord's Supper*, edited for The Parker Society by John E. Cox (Cambridge: University Press, 1844 [1580]), p. 41.
[6] Justin Martyr, *The First Apology*, in the *Writings of Saint Justin Martyr*, trans. Thomas B. Falls, The Fathers of the Church Series (New York: Christian Heritage, 1948), p. 105.
[7] John Calvin, *Institutes of the Christian Religion* (Grand Rapids: Wm. B. Eerdmans Publishing Co., 1970) Book 3, chap. 14, sec. 1, pp. 491f.
[8] *Ibid.*, Book 3, chap. 14, sec. 4, p. 492.

[9] Aurelius Augustine, *Lectures or Tractates on the Gospel According to St. John,* vol. 2, in *The Works of Aurelius Augustine,* ed. Marcus Dods, vol. 11 (Edinburgh: T. & T. Clark, 1874), Tractate 80,3, p. 300.

[10] Thayer, *Greek-English Lexicon* (Grimm) on *endunō.*

[11] Martin Luther, *The Small Catechism* (Minneapolis: Augsburg Publishing House, 1968), pp. 27-28.

[12] Cyril of Jerusalem in Paul F. Palmer, ed., *Sacraments and Worship,* Volume One, Sources of Christian Theology (Westminster, Md.: The Newman Press, 1955), p. 48.

[13] Antoine de Saint-Exupéry, *Wind, Sand and Stars,* trans. Lewis Galantiere (New York: Reynal & Hitchcock, 1939), p. 288.

[14] For those who preach from a full manuscript, a workable method of writing sermons and using the manuscript in the pulpit with a minimum of *reading* is found in Richard C. Hoefler's fine book *Creative Preaching and Oral Writing* (Lima, Ohio: C.S.S. Publishing Co., 1978).

[15] Two useful guides are William D. Thompson, *A Listener's Guide to Preaching* (Nashville: Abingdon Press, 1966), and Reuel L. Howe, *Partners in Preaching: Clergy and Laity in Dialogue* (New York: The Seabury Press, Inc., 1967).

[16] P. T. Forsyth, *Positive Preaching and the Modern Mind* (New York: Hodder & Stoughton, 1907), p. 77.

[17] Samples taken from my "Clergy and Laity: Ministry and Society," *The 99 Percenter* (New York: Episcopal Church Center), Spring, 1976.

References for Chapter Eight

[1] Quoting the paraphrase of the admonition of a psychotherapist in Harry L. Weinberg, *Levels of Knowing and Existence: Studies in General Semantics* (New York: Harper & Row, Publishers, 1959), p. 183.

[2] John Dollard and Neal E. Miller, *Personality and Psychotherapy* (New York: McGraw-Hill Book Company, 1950), p. 281 and chapter 18 passim.

[3] A. H. Maslow, *Motivation and Personality* (New York: Harper & Row, Publishers, 1954), especially chapters 5, 6, 16.

[4] Thomas C. Oden, *Kerygma and Counseling* (Philadelphia: The Westminster Press, 1966), pp. 21, 24, in italics.

[5] Gerhard von Rad, *Genesis* (Philadelphia: The Westminster Press, 1961), p. 58.

[6] *Ibid.,* p. 49.

[7] Erik H. Erikson, *Young Man Luther* (New York: W. W. Norton & Company, Inc., 1958), p. 212.

[8] "No one . . . should look for an efficient cause of an evil will, for the cause is not one of efficiency but of deficiency. . . ." *Saint Augustine, The City of God Against The Pagans,* The Loeb Classical Library (Cambridge: Harvard University Press, 1966), vol. 4, Book 12, section 7, p. 33.

[9] I am indebted to Thomas C. Oden, *The Structure of Awareness* (Nashville: Abingdon Press, 1969), for the structure of guilt, anxiety, and boredom, in relation to others, ourselves, creation, and God, in the time frame of past, future, and present.

[10] Thomas A. Harris, *I'm OK—You're OK* (New York: Harper & Row, Publishers, 1969). On page 43 he writes, "I'm not OK—You're OK . . . is the universal position of early childhood. . . ."

[11] Oden, *op. cit.,* p. 23.

[12] Eric Berne, *Games People Play* (New York: Grove Press, Inc., 1967).

[13] Harris, *op. cit.,* pp. 45-46.

[14] *Hamlet,* Act III, Scene 2.

[15] *Psychology Today,* vol. 6, no. 8 (January, 1973), p. 33. Italics mine.

[16] Robert Scheer, *How the United States Got Involved in Vietnam* (Santa Barbara: Center for the Study of Democratic Institutions, 1965).

[17] David Halberstam, *The Best and the Brightest* (New York: Random House, Inc., 1972). See p. 655, "Lyndon Johnson had lost it all, and so had the rest of them; they had, for all their brilliance and hubris and sense of themselves, been unwilling to look to and learn from the past and they had been swept forward by their belief in the importance of anti-Communism . . . and by the sense of power and glory, omnipotence and omniscience of America in this century."

[18] Edmund Bergler, *The Basic Neurosis* (New York: Grune and Stratton, Inc., 1949), p. 12.

[19] Edmund Bergler, *Principles of Self-Damage* (New York: Philosophical Library, 1959), p. 7.

[20] From "Remarks by Harold C. Morgan, M.D., to 'Business Christianity' Seminar, Trinity Parish, Columbia, South Carolina, November 23, 1969."

[21] Roland H. Bainton, *Here I Stand: A Life of Martin Luther* (New York: Abingdon-Cokesbury Press, 1950), pp. 37-46.

[22] M. Auguste Molinier, *The Thoughts of Blaise Pascal,* trans. C. Kegan Paul (London: George Bell and Sons, 1890) p. 77.

[23] Sylvia Plath, *The Bell Jar* (New York: Harper & Row, Publishers, 1971), p. 137. Used with permission of Harper & Row, Publishers, Inc.

[24] E. B. White, *Charlotte's Web* (New York: Harper &Row, Publishers, 1952), p. 114. Copyright 1952 by E. B. White. Reprinted by permission of Harper & Row, Publishers, Inc.

[25] Gerhard Kittel, ed., *Theological Dictionary of the New Testament,* trans. Geoffrey W. Bromiley (Grand Rapids: Wm. B. Eerdmans Publishing Company, 1967), vol. 4, p. 592.

[26] Allen Wheelis, *The Quest for Identity* (New York: W. W. Norton & Company, Inc., 1958), p. 19.

[27] Reinhold Niebuhr, *The Nature and Destiny of Man* (New York: Charles Scribner's Sons, 1941), vol. 1, p. 189, note 7.

[28] *Life* magazine, June 20, 1969.

[29] Ann Landers, *Washington Post,* July 31, 1969.

[30] P. T. Forsyth, *The Justification of God* (London: Independent Press, 1948 [1917]), p. 127.

[31] *Ladies' Home Journal,* November, 1966, p. 97.

[32] From a review of *Ex-pastors: Why Men Leave the Parish Ministry* by Gerald J. Jud, Edgar W. Mills, Jr., and Genevieve W. Burch (Boston: Pilgrim Press, 1970), in the "Professional Supplement" to *The Episcopalian.*

[33] *Newsweek,* March 26, 1973.

[34] Wheelis, *op. cit.,* p. 88.

[35] Reported in *Parade,* May 11, 1975, p. 12.

[36] Werner Graf, quoted in Henry Allen, "The Fascination of Boredom," *Potomac* Magazine, August 18, 1974, page 36.

[37] Søren Kierkegaard, *Either/Or,* trans. David F. Swenson and Lillian Marvin Swenson (Princeton: Princeton University Press, 1944), vol. 1, pp. 234-237.

[38] *Ibid.,* pp. 237-240.
[39] *Ibid.,* p. 240.
[40] *Ibid.,* p. 242.
[41] *Ibid.,* p. 239.
[42] "The Thrill Seekers," *Newsweek,* August 18, 1975.
[43] Arthur Miller, "The Bored and the Violent," *Harper's,* November, 1962.
[44] Kittell, *op. cit.,* vol. 4, p. 522.
[45] My interpretation of Galatians 6:9, using the Greek and Thayer's lexicon.
[46] John Calvin, *Institutes of the Christian Religion* (Grand Rapids: Wm. B. Eerdmans Publishing Company, 1970), Book 3, chap. 9, sec. 1, p. 26.
[47] *Ibid.,* sec. 4, p. 28.
[48] *Ibid.,* sec. 6, pp. 34-35.
[49] Karl Barth, *The Epistle to the Romans* (London: Oxford University Press, 1933), p. 428.
[50] C. K. Barrett, *A Commentary on the Epistle to the Romans* (New York: Harper & Row, Publishers, 1957), p. 231.
[51] Oden, *op. cit.* pp. 188-189: "We count it [boredom] to be *the* essential form of the predicament of man in the present."

INDEX

whole of, 165
guilt (see sin)

hermeneutics
doctrines of, 72-75
issues of, 71-72
model of, 81-85
process of, 75-76, 85-86
schema of, 80-81
theology and, 79
hope (see gospel)

image, 126

language
behavior and, 117-122, 145
as 'map,' 27-31, 54, 65, 81-85
perception and, 117-122, 145
silence and, 129
therapy and, 146
Word of God, 74-75, 129-130
word study, 65-66
liturgy
of Christ, 128-129
of church in world, 141-144
of church in worship (see worship)
meanings of, 127-128
love (see gospel)

'map' (see language)
movement in sermon (see dynamics)

new results
of gospel (see gospel: results of)
of preaching (see preaching: results of)
in sermon (see dynamics: Dynamic Factors in sermon)

persons: preacher and congregation
biblical understanding of, 17-18
as church gathered, 36, 129, 140-141

as church scattered, 36-38, 141-144
communication and perception complex, 130-133
doctrine of, 73-74
dynamics of change, 112-116
fear of preacher, 88
identification (That's me and Thank God), 15, 18, 26, 53-54, 56-67, 65, 113
multilevel, multimedia, 130-133
perception and communication, 130-133
preacher as listener and messenger, 38
word-perception-behavior, 17-18, 116-123
points (see Synopsis)
preacher (see persons)
preaching
anguish of, 19
audacity of, 129
church's role in, 36, 140-141
content of, 18-19
designing the sermon, 31-33
idealistic, 17-18, 20-21, 33, 116, 117, 122
method, 16
moralistic, 17-18, 20-21, 33, 37-38, 73-74, 100, 114, 116, 117, 122
pastoral concern, 111
power of, 23-25, 112
results of, 34-38, 116, 132-133, 154, 158-159, 163-164
structure of sermon, 19
telling delivery, 25-26, 137-140

resulting consequences
in sermon (see dynamics: Dynamic Factors in sermon)
of sin (see sin: result of)
root
in sermon (see dynamics: Dynamic Factors in sermon)
of sin (see sin)